Your Quest For Spiritual Knowledge

To Prepare You For
Two Thousand and Twelve
and Beyond
... and Empower Yourself

Your Quest For Spiritual Knowledge

To Prepare You For
Two Thousand and Twelve
and Beyond
... and Empower Yourself

Michelle Corrigan

BOOKS

Winchester, UK
Washington, USA

First published by O-Books, 2011
O Books is an imprint of John Hunt Publishing Ltd., The Bothy, Deershot Lodge, Park Lane, Ropley,
Hants, SO24 0BE, UK
office1@o-books.net
www.o-books.com

For distributor details and how to order please visit the 'Ordering' section on our website.

Text copyright: Michelle Corrigan 2009

ISBN: 978 1 84694 417 8

A CIP catalogue record for this book is available from the British Library.

Design: Stuart Davies

Printed in the UK by CPI Antony Rowe
Printed in the USA by Offset Paperback Mfrs, Inc

We operate a distinctive and ethical publishing philosophy in all
areas of its business, from its global network of authors to
production and worldwide distribution.

CONTENTS

Introduction   1

About the Author   3

Chapter One -   What is happening out there?   5

Chapter Two -   How can you change?   10

Chapter Three -   The Chakras   21

Chapter Four -   Energy Healing   41

Chapter Five -   Sacred Texts   50

Chapter Six -   Numerology   67

Chapter Seven -   Tarot - the Journey of Life   81

Chapter Eight -   Aromatherapy   106

Chapter Nine -   Crystals   113

Chapter Ten -   Shamanism   122

Chapter Eleven -   Death   138

Chapter Twelve -   Nutrition   141

Chapter Thirteen -   The Bigger Picture - The Environment
                     and The Universe   143

Chapter Fourteen - An Article on Thinking   146

I would like to dedicate this book to my beautiful Mother, born on 7th February 1927, who passed away on 23rd September 2009 and to my Father, born on 17th January 1919, who holds great values in life and who has the most incredible strength.

Introduction

I felt this book was needed to help people understand what is happening on Planet Earth up to 2012 and beyond. There are great changes taking place. Vibrations are rising which means connecting your own energy with that of the Great Divine. The human race can become more unified by taking simple measures.

The following guidance will prepare you for these changes and will help you to be aware of what you can do personally, for the environment, for the Planet, for the Universe. We, as a human race, are risking extinction with our lack of respect for ourselves, each other and Mother Earth. Many live in ignorance of their own consciousness, let alone the concept of the Collective Consciousness.

This book will reassure you that this is not a time to have fears and dreads but is a time for peace and harmony. It is an end to these turbulent times of disillusion, suffering, unhappiness, and over-activity of the mental energy - the mind.

Active awareness is the key.

There is no great mystery to what is written here, this is a way of life.

Personally I have found the knowledge contained in this book has changed my life and opened up a world of seeking and self-discovery. This had led to knowing who I am and my true purpose in life. The spiritual path can be 'as sharp as a razor's edge' and it is often tempting to diversify and 'go off to the sides'. But if you know your purpose and can balance all aspects of your life, then you will reach liberation of suffering, you will have self-realizations, and you will become enlightened.

This book will help you to:

~ Learn about Self Empowerment

1

~ Learn about the energy shifts that are happening
~ Connect with an energy higher than the Self
~ Understand the spiritual Self
~ Understand the difference between knowledge and wisdom
~ Understand the need to shift blocked energy within the body
~ Understand The Spirit World
~ Understand the chakras and esoteric body
~ Learn how to shift blocked energy physically emotionally and spiritually
~ Learn how to Meditate
~ Learn how Tools such as Tarot, Crystals, Meditation, Shamanic Journey and Soul Retrieval can help you
~ Find peace in your mind
~ Make changes to lifestyle
~ Appreciate life
~ Develop the mind
~ Live with awareness

About the Author

My Yoga journey began many moons ago in 1994 while on a two-year expatriate spell in Bangkok. I often visited the beautiful Thai Buddhist temples and went on a Meditation retreat run by Buddhist Monks which was in the form of Vipassana Meditation - insight meditation focusing on the breath and repeating mantras (sacred sounds) on the rise and fall of the abdomen. While in Bangkok, I also studied Thai massage - a wonderful body treatment whereby the energy lines are pressed with the thumbs and palms of the hands.

I then trained as an Aromatherapist in Dorking, England, which is a lovely body massage using bespoke aromatherapy oils, tracing meridians, making this a holistic treatment.

While living in Devon I trained as a Reiki Practitioner, which introduced me to the esoteric body system. I also joined a meditation group which helped me with expanding the technique of visualization and opened up my spiritual awareness.

In 2002, I moved to Surrey with my family and set up my own meditation and healing groups, and in 2004 I started my training with the British Wheel of Yoga as a Yoga Teacher.

I believe that once you are working with energies in ways such as Reiki, this 'opens up' the spiritual channels. While doing a spiritual reading with my Teacher, I started to 'channel' which means that Spirit works through me to channel philosophy. This is to spread 'the word' to as many people as possible in order for a better balance to come back to them.

I realized that my path is to do deep soul work and seek liberation, so I have also spent time doing self-study and healing. I have spent some years looking at the Self, discovering who I am, my purpose for being here and healing at a soul level. I have found all the Tools mentioned in this book such as Shamanic

Healing, Tarot, Crystals, Reiki and Numerology   really life-changing.

My Sanskrit name, given to me by my great Yoga tutor Swami Satchidananda Mataji, is "Mokshapriya" which means "She for whom liberation is dear". In numerology, I am a number 5 which means I am here to do Soul work and work as a Master Healer and Spiritual Teacher, to pass on the higher truth.

My first non-fiction book *Your Quest for a Spiritual Life* is also published by O-Books and I have recorded a Meditation CD *Your Quest for Peace, Healing & Balance.*

Please visit my website at www.purplebuddha.co.uk

Chapter 1

What is Happening Out There?

There are great shifts in energy taking place. It has been happening for years and will continue gradually up until the beginning of 2012 and beyond. Although, at the start of 2012 there will be a significant shift, the vibration will be felt particularly by those who are in tune with universal energies. They are those evolved Souls and who in this life have been working on the Self in the form of self-development, healing their wounds, shedding their mental and emotional baggage. These people will already be feeling the change. Many challenges and lessons have come, and are coming, their way.

At the time of the Winter Solstice at 11.11am on 21st December 2012, there will be a rare astrological configuration of planets, which happens every 26,000 years.

The Individual will feel what can be described as a surge of energy. Midnight on 31st December 2011 will be a potent time to meditate, that is midnight your local time.

Let us be positive and view this as an exciting time for change; that is what it can be. Some rather bleakly view this time as the end of civilization, the end of the world, but it is in fact a new beginning. Do not be afraid, but be aware. This is a wonderful potential to make a very different world. This time has been predicted by many cultures who have continued practicing the old ways, such as The Mayans and the Incas. This is a chance to change the way that people live. Up until this time people have been led by money, power and ego. This as a whole cannot be sustained. Money as an energy has got out of hand. Money is needed to pay bills, keep families in their homes, and to enable them to drive their cars but money should not be the driving force. Where have contentment, happiness and joy gone? Life should no longer be about striving for the biggest and the best in the material world and judgment of success should not be assessed by how much your house is worth or what car you drive. Happiness comes from love in the heart, for the Self, family and friends, our four legged animal friends, and the environment - the beauty of nature.

Life could become more simple. Work could be enjoyed and not taken on just for the money. Families could come together more - eat together, communicate and, like the old ways, be part of a family in the community. This has been lost over the years. Neighbors could assist each other, not be in feuds over trivialities such as a foot of fence line, parking, etc. This is a time for people to come together, to not be selfish, to find their feminine, nurturing, caring side and use this for themselves and to be compassionate to others.

The veil between the two worlds of earth and spirit will become closer. A portal will open up for us as human beings to enter on an energy level. This portal can be viewed as new energy.

Ego will no longer lead the human race and instead higher truths and inner wisdom will take over. This is a chance to end severe suffering and karmic actions. Humans can pull together but there are many who will resist this and they must be made aware of their ignorance.

By spreading love and compassion those in the dark will eventually see the light, but there is much work to do for those in the know and this can be broken down into the following categories:

~ Personal work - be in touch with the spiritual Self, get back your Power
~ Environmental work - respect the environment, recycle, preserve energy

~ Universal work - forming and attending groups with like-minded people, sending out the right intent, healing and love, and meditating alone - 12.00 noon is said to be a powerful time

Male / Female Energies
The Great Goddess

Female power has been suppressed over thousands of years. The male energy of ego has dominated the female energies of intuition, wisdom, higher truths, nurturing, compassion and kindness.

Now it is time for the Goddess within to be born again. We all have male and female energies within and a balance of both will bring harmony.

We need male energy within us for confidence, but too much will result in an over-inflated ego and too little will result in low self-esteem.

We need female energy within us so we can work intuitively, nurture ourselves and others, and be compassionate.

The dominance of male energy has resulted in conflict and wars over the years.

This time of the Goddess may perhaps lead to less knowledge, but more wisdom. People will lead more simple lives and times will become less turbulent and more settled across the Planet Earth.

Balance

Yin and Yang are complementary opposites within a greater whole. One cannot exist without the other. The shape of Yin and Yang represents interaction of the two energies, black for Yin and

white for Yang. They are not entirely black or white just as things in life are not entirely black or white.

You will be able to see from the above where balance is needed of both energies. This can also be applied to many aspects of life. Spiritually, the balance is needed in our energy in the Chakras (the seven energy centers within the body, please see chapter 3). We need to be grounded first - connected to Mother Earth, feeling the energy from our own Base, Sacral, and Solar Plexus Chakras connecting to the beautiful Earth energies. Then the love of our Heart Center can be balanced and the links from our upper centers, the Throat, Brow and Crown Chakras, can be made with Spirit.

In life generally a balance of spiritual energies and the material energies is needed to be in harmony, which means working on the Self, being in touch intuitively and also being in touch with the material world of work, family, money, home, etc.

Sun energy

The Sun energy is related to Male, Yang energy which is light; opposite to dark energy. The Sun gives us vitality and is related to the element of fire and this gives us active energy. We need this energy to give us the 'get up and go'. See it like stoking a fire, give the fire fuel and it will burn brightly. No fuel and it will burn out. On a physical level Sun energy within us corresponds to our sympathetic nervous system. Ego is male energy which is connected to our center of Fire - the Solar Plexus. This is who we are as an individual personality. The Ego rules the mind until you find union with the Lunar energy, where intuition and wisdom will dominate.

Moon energy

The Moon energy within us is our feminine, goddess energy, Yin energy. Whereas the Solar Plexus is linked to the Sun, the Lunar Plexus which is situated in the cerebrum is linked to The Moon.

She is our intuitive side, our unconscious, and is linked to the element of water - our emotions. This energy corresponds to our parasympathetic nervous system on a physical level, our calming energy.

The cycle of the Moon is the same length of time as the female menstrual cycle - 28 days. The Moon has three phases - waxing, full and waning. The Moon at one time was worshipped as a powerful force and her energy effects water tides. The planting of seeds and crops would have been done at a certain phase of the Moon, as well as harvesting.

By tuning into the cycles and phases of the moon, we can become more harmonious. It is interesting to follow our own emotional ups and downs alongside the changes in the moon.

Chapter 2

How Can You Change?

In starting out there is much personal work to do. There are many already who are prepared and able to help and they must carry on with their good work of healing, Soul work, and practicing spirituality. Individuals should not be ignorant of their spiritual sides.

The following points would make a good start:

~ Start making changes *now*
~ Start by making changes to your physical energy - think about some form of shifting energy such as Yoga, T'ai Chi orChi Quong
~ Learn how to breathe efficiently and properly (see 'Breathing' at the end of this Chapter)
~ Meditate to calm the mind
~ Study sacred texts such as The Yoga Sutras - they are the foundation of all knowledge
~ Healing - study the self, get to know the essence of the real you, work at healing your wounds - letting go. This could mean finding a teacher, going to a therapist, seeking.

What is spirituality?

Let us look at humans - spirit in a physical body with a soul that has had many lives. Always looking outside the self for joy, fun, laughter, love and guidance.

If you are religious, going to your place of worship and reading the sacred scripts does not necessarily make you a spiritual person. The essence of religions is spiritual, but unfortunately has been lost in many cases.

If you help others and send your money to charities, but neglect your own nurturing and self love, then this will make you a beautiful person, but not necessarily a spiritual soul.

Those on their spiritual path will tend to respect their physical body. They will know the Self because they will have followed a healing path, nurturing the self, healing their wounds and working on their own suffering and issues, not suppressing them. This person will be connected to the Soul and therefore gain access to true wisdom and truths. Those on their spiritual path tend to spend time quietening the mind by practicing meditation.

A spiritual person will practice what they preach, which means they will take what they learn from their spiritual practices into their daily lives.

They will have had and will continue to have tyrants in their lives - those that will teach them in such a way that, at the time, the experience could be traumatic such as a confrontation, an over-opinionated person, an over-powering relationship, those that think they are always right or do not listen to anyone else's point of view and so on.

Recognizing traits in others that are often mirroring qualities in the self such as those just mentioned, plus anger for instance, but on the other end of the scale seeing beautiful qualities in others that are hidden in the Self such as inner beauty, peace, inner power and knowledge. Patterns and karmic behavior will be studied through the family and broken and cleared by the Healer (either the Self or a Therapist). These patterns could be issues such as control, anger, addictions, an inability to express emotions, traits and habits.

Then, they will become a purer channel and spirit can work with them which means now they have helped themselves, they are ready to help others. Their light will shine within and this beautiful balanced energy and pure divine love will emanate to others, the environment and the Planet, and the Universe.

Unlocking wisdom and gaining access to higher truths can be done in the following ways:

The Soul

The Soul is the spiritual essence of who we are. The Soul is said to be situated around the heart and Solar Plexus area but you could say that the soul is in every cell. The Soul is everlasting - the Soul will be reincarnated, will experience many lives. Through these incarnations the soul will become 'whole' and complete. We come into each incarnation with a certain destiny, certain things to learn, certain experiences to have. We are born into a family and certain environment where we can learn these lessons. We 'choose' a certain life where we can be enriched by these experiences so we can evolve spiritually.

We are made up of the following qualities/energies:

~ Parents - their genes, characteristics, way they bring us up, conditioned thoughts
   Date of birth - astrology - planets, horoscope, sun sign, moon sign, ascendant
      - numerology - date of birth - destiny number (see Chapter 6)
      - elements: Air, Water, Fire, Earth, Ether

To quote from Juan Mascaro's translation of *The Bhaghavad Gita* (sacred Sanskrit text) - Chapter 7 verse 4 - 'The visible forms of my nature are eight: earth, water, fire, air, ether, the mind, reason, and the sense of 'I'.'

To keep it simple, think of us as Spirit, with a physical body. Within the physical body are the elements just mentioned.

Have you ever thought 'What is my Soul journey for this life? What is my purpose? Who are my Soul mates - the ones that I learn from the most?'

Verses that explain the soul from *The Baghavad Gita*

Death and reincarnation from chapter 2:

Verse 13) 'As the Spirit of our mortal body wanders on in childhood, and youth and old age, the Spirit wanders on to a new body: of this the sage has no doubts.'

Verse 17) 'Interwoven in his creation, the Spirit is beyond destruction. No one can bring to an end the Spirit which is everlasting.'

Spirit is immortal.

(So the physical body is left behind and the soul then goes into the spirit world, ready to reincarnate.)

The soul lives in the Spirit World (sometimes known as the 'Devaloka') until it is time to return.

Verse 20) 'He is never born, and he never dies, He is in Eternity: he is for evermore. Never-born and eternal, beyond times gone or to come, he does not die when the body dies.'

The Soul does not die when the body dies.

Verse 22) 'As a man leaves an old garment and puts on one that is new, the Spirit leaves his mortal body and then puts on one that is new.'

We incarnate, new life, new lessons (or re-learn old lessons if we did not learn from experiences in the first place).

Map of soul journey

Earthly energies are as follows:

You are BORN

You go through CHILDHOOD

You grow into ADULTHOOD

You may have a partner and children and have your own FAMILY

You work and develop your CAREER

You get ESTABLISHED MATERIALLY - MONEY, HOUSE

You become aware of your health and PHYSICAL BODY - NUTRITION, LIFESTYLE

These are all your EARTHLY ENERGIES

Spiritual energies

AT SOME STAGE YOU BECOME AWARE THAT THERE IS MORE TO LIFE THAN THE MATERIAL WORLD:

CHANGES OCCUR

You start to develop BODY DISCIPLINE, MIND CONTROL AND MEDITATION

You FOLLOW your SPIRITUAL PATH

Your ATTITUDE TO OTHERS CHANGES

Your ATTITUDE TO THE SELF CHANGES

You RESPECT THE PHYSICAL BODY WITH GOOD NUTRITION AND EXERCISE understanding that this will help you later in life as you grow older

You MEDITATE and develop UNION WITH THE SELF AND GREAT DIVINE

You may experience SAMADHI – A UNITIVE STATE BEYOND MIND, BLISSFUL STATE OF BEING, COMPLETE TRANSCENDENCE OF IDENTIFICATION WITH THE PERSONAL EGO

You APPLY THESE TEACHINGS TO SELF AND OTHERS IN DAILY LIFE AS A BEING. You STAY GROUNDED, stay CONNECTED. UNDERSTAND SOUL JOURNEY, your PURPOSE in life.

The GOALS are - SELF REALIZATION. LIBERATION. ENLIGHTENMENT.

These are your SPIRITUAL ENERGIES

The following are extracts from *The Bhagavad Gita* - an ancient Indian text:

Chapter 4 Verse 38) 'Because there is nothing like wisdom which can make us pure on this earth. The man who lives in self-harmony finds this truth in his soul.'

(We learn from sacred books, Gurus and Masters and we decipher these teachings into our own truths.)

Chapter 5 Verse 11) 'The Yogi works for the purification of the soul: he throws off selfish attachment, and thus it is only his body or his senses or his mind or his reason that works.'

(We are here to purify the Soul - through the vows of life, the Yamas and Niyamas (the sacred vows of life, attitude to self and to the outside world- Kriya Yoga - body discipline, mind control and meditation) (see chapter 5, Sacred Texts).

Chapter 6 Verse 6) 'The soul of man is his friend when by the Spirit he has conquered his soul; but when a man is not lord of his soul then this becomes his own enemy."

Darkness, unhappiness, inertia. (These people are 'Lost Souls' way out of touch with the Self).

Chapter 6 Verse 7-13) 'Meditation - spend time in solitude, master of his mind, hoping for nothing, desiring nothing, finding peace.'

Chapter 6 Verse 19) 'Then his soul is a lamp whose light is steady, for it burns in a shelter where no winds come.

Soul becomes in union with the Great Divine. Soul is pure, attains perfection through many lives and reaches the "End Supreme.'

Summary of the Soul

We are spirit in a physical body. Through the disciplines of following a spiritual path we can achieve self-realization - find out who we are, our purpose, find liberation from conditioning, attachments, desires, suffering and find our truth, happiness and love. Through spiritual practice we can escape the never ending cycle of births and deaths. We can put a stop to Karma (see Chapter 5, Sacred Texts, Practice and Discipline). We can awaken or re-awaken the Soul - our own identity as the 'spiritual' Self.

References: *The Bhagavad Gita* - Juan Mascaro

Sometimes it is easier to understand things by seeing the Soul as the essence, the center. This center then gets layered by our emotions and our mental baggage. Often the symbology used is an onion. The layers of the onion are peeled off to reveal the center as our layers of emotional and mental blockages are removed to get to the Soul. Our spiritual body (also known as causal body or esoteric body) is made up of the Chakras and channels within. Within our energy system the 'samskaras' are contained, these are the subtle impressions of all the lives that you have lived.

At the time of death the soul and spirit leave the physical body, when the last breath is taken.

In a blissful, liberated, enlightened state, the soul and spirit are in complete union.

Who needs Healing?

Just about all human beings.

As you travel your journey of life, you will probably gather some 'baggage'. This baggage can be emotional or mental. Emotionally we hang on to our traumas and this energy is often blocking the Heart Chakra which may lead to physical disease of the heart. Deep old childhood issues are stored in the Sacral Chakra. Healing in its various forms can unblock this energy. Old wounds and traumas are stored in our memory and the cells of the body and unless the blockages are healed, this can manifest in the physical body in the form of illness and disease.

Forms of healing:

Spiritual healing such as Reiki, Crystal Healing, Energy Healing
    Talking therapies with a Spiritual Listener
    Shamanic Healing
    Yoga - following the Eight Limbs
    Meditation
    Obtaining spiritual guidance either from someone already on the path who has experience, or through communing with your Spirit Guides

Practicing some form of exercise to shift energy

The most spiritual form of physical exercise is Yoga, T'ai Chi, or Chi Quong, but of course there are also the aerobic-type exercises such as running and cycling. These aerobic exercises will certainly shift energy and keep you physically fit, which is positive, but is not quite the same as working spiritually. Quite often these forms of physical exercise are just to keep the physical body in shape and can sometimes be more about feeding the ego than anything else. The most environmentally friendly form of aerobic exercise would be to cycle where possible rather than take a car.

Yoga postures will work on strength and flexibility and by stretching the muscles this will release toxins and emotional stress that the body holds onto in the cells of muscles and body tissue. Working aerobically cannot achieve this.

It is advisable to go to an experienced and qualified Yoga teacher rather than trying to learn the postures yourself at home.

Each posture has a Sanskrit name which in itself carries a certain energy.

Yoga is spiritual because it works on the body, mind and spirit.

When doing the postures it is more effective to shift energy to work with the breath, to use the breath as your focus, along with the movement and where in the body you can feel the posture working. An example would be a Triangle, known in Sanskrit as Trikonasana. You prepare your mind for the posture. You take your feet a good three feet apart, you turn out your right foot and raise your arms to shoulder height with the palms facing down on an inhale. As you exhale, you lean sideways to the right and then take the posture fully by lowering the right arm, hand on shin, and extending the left arm up. You stay in the posture, breathing using the full capacity of your lungs. When your breathing starts to change, or your body is telling you to come out the posture, do so with care and attention.

Yoga calms the mind and concentration begins as soon as you are on your mat. Your mind should be focused as you take your practice and should not wander onto other things other than the breath, the movement of the posture and body awareness.

If you go to a class, then do not think that once a week is enough, although that said you will still feel some benefits. Ideally, you need self-discipline to practice on a daily basis. This could be a goal to aim towards.

A good Yoga class will also teach you breathing techniques known as Pranayama and Meditation, these are an equally important part of your practice.

While practicing Yoga postures you should be alert but comfortable and if you go to a class where your body is screaming at you in pain from overexertion, then listen to what your body is trying to tell you. You may have to try out several classes. Listen to your intuition and see how you feel after your class. You should feel calm and relaxed but at the same time feel as if you have more energy. There are some who think that Yoga postures are just another form of physical exercise but there is more depth to Yoga than just having a beautiful body.

There is no doubt that having a toned body is a lovely bonus of practicing Yoga, but this should not be the goal, it is far beyond that.

Your teacher should send out lovely positive vibes, because in theory they should be someone who you admire and aspire to be like. But at the same time, if you idolize another person which could be your Teacher or a Guru for instance, be aware of not giving them your power. That is not good for either of you. Practice discernment when choosing your teacher.

Breathing

Impurities are exhaled through the breath. Practicing breathing techniques will help to shift blocked energy and will expel toxins.

It is quite amazing how we take our breathing totally for

granted and how little we know and understand about how to breathe properly. For instance, after the inhale, there is a natural pause and also after the exhale, there is a natural pause.

Do you even know what is happening in the body when you breathe?

When you inhale, observe the following:

~ feel the ribcage expanding out to the side
~ feel the chest open
~ feel the abdomen rising, or expanding outwards
~ the diaphragm lowers

When you exhale, observe the following:

~ feel the ribcage coming back in
~ feel the abdomen and chest falling, or coming inwards
~ the diaphragm rises

We normally breathe around 14-16 breaths per minute. By focusing on breathing techniques it is possible to greatly reduce the breaths per minute, which is very healing, calming for the mind and body, will reduce stress, will reduce blood pressure and is anti-ageing!

Prana is energy and is also known as Chi or Ki. Prana is our life force and is in the air we breathe, the food we eat and in the drinks we consume.

Exercise to Observe the Breath

Observe your breathing this time and follow the length of each breath, breathing in and out through the nose:

Watch the inhale, watch the exhale.
See that there is a natural pause after the inhale and after the exhale.

Breathe to the full length of your breath.

Inhale pure energy, exhale impurities.

Everything around you is energy - things you see such as people, animals, plants.

There are energy centers below you, above you and within you. The seven main centers within are known as the Chakras. These centers form the subtle body.

Exercise in Retention of the Breath

Retention of the breath brings absolute stillness to the mind and body.

An example would be:

Inhale for count of 6

Hold for count of 3

Exhale for count of 6

Hold for count of 3

The mind is then fixed on the breath and is in preparation for Meditation.

Exercise in Observing Your Breath on an Energy Level

As you inhale through the nose, visualize healing energy in the form of a gold light coming in the nostrils. Watch this golden light coming in the nostrils, and down the chest, down the abdomen to the base of the body.

Pause.

As you exhale, visualize tension leaving the body.

Pause.

Repeat several times.

Practice a meditation purely focusing on your breath, observing the breath and watching the breath settle.

Chapter 3

The Seven Energy Centers Known as Chakras

Chakra is a Sanskrit word meaning 'wheel of energy'. When the Chakra is healthy and balanced the energy will spin round. When there are disturbances to the physical body, emotions or mind, the center becomes blocked. These blockages occur as you go through life and experience traumas whether they be physical, emotional or mental - however you perceive them to be.

Around your body is your energy field, your aura. Your chakras are linked to this energy field with vibrations. All around you is energy, spirit, light. As you peel off your layers of blocked emotions and negative thoughts, your energy field expands and becomes clear of these blockages; your light gets brighter. Your chakras will shine like beautiful jewels. Some people can see these energy colors.

The individual Self becomes whole. Your lower chakras link to the earth energies and your upper chakras (from the heart upwards) link to spirit energies. Your sense of seeing, taste, hearing, touching and smelling develops. In time these senses will be used not only on the earth plane but when you are linked in to the spirit plane

There are also several chakras below us and several above our Crown. The seven Chakras within are related to our development age in life, to parts of the body and the endocrine system.

Base Chakra - Mooladhara
The base chakra is usually seen as an earthy red color and is known as the Mooladhara. This word means 'root'. It is situated

at the very base of the spine. The developmental age for this center is from birth to around 3-4 years of age. This means that your base chakra relates to experiences during this age range, for example it will be effected by how your birth into this life was, the energy in your family - was this a loving environment or quite the opposite? These are the first few years of your life from birth to a toddler.

This center is very much about your grounding energy - how you connect in life to the material world, money, work, and more naturally to nature itself. Are you a grounded person or are you someone who likes to flit around, not noticing nature, with your head in the clouds?

This chakra also relates to the sexual function of your body, it can be affected by your attitude to the self and your own self respect, as well as your attitude to others and your sexual behaviour.

The Sacral Chakra - Svadhistana

The sacral chakra is usually seen as an orange energy and is known as Svadhistana. It is situated below the navel. The developmental age for this center is between 4 to around 8-9 which is a significant time in life as your first day at school will be experienced, a time when you start to have some independence from parents. These years are spent playing and learning, gaining early social skills.

The Sacral Chakra is also linked to grounding energies. We store deep emotions in this center and often hold on to unnecessary past issues. The reproductive organs are linked to this center and it is said that once this center is cleansed that creative energy will be released.

The lower digestive tract is linked to this center and often those who have deep emotional wounds will suffer with small intestine problems and bowel issues.

The Solar Plexus Chakra - Manipura

The solar plexus chakra is usually seen as bright yellow and is known as Manipura. It is situated around the stomach area. The developmental age for this center is from around 8-9 to the teenage years around 13. An age when most leave junior school behind and move into senior school. For some who have confidence, this can be an exciting time but for those who lack self-esteem and confidence it can be a very fearful time.

Solar meaning Sun, this center is often called the center of fire. Too much of this energy will result in over confidence, inflated ego and high opinions of the Self but too little will result in low self-esteem, lack of confidence and low self-opinion so a good balance is needed.

Physically this center is linked to the digestive system. Often those who are overly anxious or suffer from stress will suffer from digestive problems. If stress is under control then the digestive system can be healthy.

The Heart Chakra - Anahata

The heart chakra is usually seen as a beautiful green or pink energy and is known as Anahata. It is situated around the heart area. The developmental age for this center is from around 13 years of age to around 18 years of age, the years of falling in love and falling out of love which very much affects the heart energy.

By connecting with The Great Divine negative emotions and blocked energy can be cleared. Some will be lucky enough to experience a connection where they feel the bliss of pure divine love.

The Heart Chakra is seen as the point where energies meet - the three grounding energies of Base, Sacral and Solar Plexus and the three spiritual energies of the Throat, Brow and Crown. To experience pure divine love, you have to learn how to give love as well as accept love and also love the self.

Clairsentience is where your senses of feeling are heightened and you can feel spirit around you as well as within you.

The Throat Chakra - Visuddha

The throat chakra is usually seen as a blue energy. It is known as Visuddha. It is situated around the throat area. The developmental age for this center is from around 18 years to around 21 years of age.

This is the center of communication - how we express ourselves, how we listen. Blocked communication will result in blockages in the throat center which physically come in the form of throat problems, thyroid issues and neck problems.

This is one of the upper spiritual centers and when communication skills of listening and speaking are heightened then clairaudience may be a gift bestowed upon you. Clairaudience is the gift of being able to hear Spirit for you to communicate messages of support and guidance to help others.

The Brow Chakra - Ajna

The brow chakra is usually seen as indigo or purple energy and is known as Ajna. It is situated above the nose around the brow area. The developmental age for this center is from around 21 years of age upwards with no limit. This is the center of clairvoyance, the art of seeing with the eyes closed. Some can see Spirit and can convey messages from lost loved ones to those in need of guidance and support. Evidence can be given of the spirit world.

This center, being in the head, is linked to the mind - our friend and our enemy. Often if someone suffers from headaches it is because of mental stress - an overactive mind and lack of positive perception. This is where meditation would be particularly useful - to calm this energy down, bringing peace to the mind.

The Crown Chakra - Sahasrara

The crown chakra is usually seen as white or violet or gold energy and is known as Sahasrara - the thousand petaled lotus flower. It is situated on the top of the head. There is no developmental age for this Chakra, all ages of life affect this center.

The Crown is the center where Spirit can link and if this center is blocked then links will be weak and maybe the person could be too grounded and therefore oblivious to their spiritual nature. If this center is too open and the grounding centers are blocked then this person would struggle in the material world of work and responsibilities because they are likely to have their head in the clouds and like the pink and fluffy world that is up there.

The Spirit World

By actively practicing physical energy work, meditation and healing your wounds, you will start to peel off layers of baggage and you may start to sense, feel or see the spirit world which can come in many forms:

- ~ Feeling a sense of being in touch with a bigger energy or light
- ~ Loved ones in spirit, either sensing or seeing and maybe connecting with them
- ~ Spirit Guides - those in light who come to you to guide and protect. Guides often come in forms such as Native Americans, Elders and Wise Ones from across the World, such as Shamans, Monks and Nuns
- ~ Power Animals - animal Spirit friends who come to guide and protect you
- ~ Earthlings - Faeries, Elves and little Earth Beings
- ~ Angels and Archangels
- ~ Ascended Masters

Spirit will only link to you when you are ready. Spirit can link to you through the practice of meditation and active awareness.

Spirit can come through on any of the above dimensions depending on what level you are on - this depends on your self and your own development and awareness, your studies, your wisdom. Spirit will only link to you if your intentions are pure; for guidance and support to the self and those in need.

If you see your Spirit Guide in your Meditations or dream world then trust what you are seeing and work with this energy for your Guide will help you, protect your energy and once you connect, you will be able to commune and seek guidance.

Guides will come and go and like anything, do not become attached to and reliant upon them. Some may stick with you, some may move on and allow new Guides to step in and this will depend on what 'work' you are doing.

Do not worry if you do not see you Guides and beware of those people who are in ego and tell you what powerful, high energies they are working with.

How to Ground your Energies

Before trying to link with the Spirit World, it is vital to be grounded first. Simply feel your feet on the ground and try and see actual roots coming out of your feet into Mother Earth before doing any energy work. When you walk, feel each step you take.

Go out into nature and actually touch trees, feel their energy, and spend some time in this environment.

Visualize a white light coming down into your Crown. Pull this white light down through each Chakra, down your legs and into the Earth, seeing roots going deep into the ground.

Another way would be to take a deep breath up from Mother Earth and visualize the energy coming up into your Base Chakra. Bring this energy up through each Chakra until you come to the Crown. Bring this energy through the Crown and then see the energy fall back down the sides of your body, like a fountain, back into Mother Earth.

If at any time, you feel ungrounded then breathe up grounding energies from Mother Earth, actually touch a tree or sit with your back leaning on the trunk or watch some trash TV!

Find a 'sit spot' out in nature which could be in a forest, sitting on a fallen tree and just 'being'. This means being in the present, feeling the energy beneath you, seeing the Plant World around you, seeing the wildlife, taking it all in.

Protection

It is important not only to ground your energies, but also to protect your energies. This is to stop your own energies leaking from your Chakras and Aura and also to stop any negative energies coming in whether this negative energy is from another person, the environment or from the Spirit World. Some do not believe it is necessary to protect their energy as they want to mirror themselves into others and vice versa and welcome the challenges this will bring. These people go about their daily lives 'open'. For those who are beginners to energy work and those who are particularly sensitive perhaps it is a good idea to protect energies. This can be done as follows:

* Visualize yourself in a bubble of protective white light
* Visualize a spiral of light from the head to the toes
* Visualize a purple cloak upon you
* See protective symbols at the front of your body around your heart, the rear at   the heart, and at each side
* See a shield in front of you
* Ask your Spirit Guides for protection
* Close down your Chakras and imagine your Aura close to your body
* When you have finished doing energy work such as healing, Yoga, Meditation etc, take your hands to the side of your body, take a deep breath in and raise   y o u r

arms above your head. Sweep your hands down the front of your body and say 'Finish'. Repeat this three times

Meditation

There are many different techniques of meditation and I think it is best to try many different ways of meditating and find the one that suits you best.

With regards to position of your body, as to whether you sit or lie down, traditionally in the East the seated posture is used for Meditation, preferably cross-legged on the floor. To make this more comfortable, use a cushion under the sitting bones for support, or a Yoga block. The important point is to be comfortable. Yogis would sit in the Lotus posture, but cross-legged is fine. Obviously if this is not suitable, then sit comfortably in a chair. The idea is that you do not fall asleep. By practicing Meditation seated, the Kundalini energy can rise up the channels, taking this spiritual energy from the Base chakra up to the Crown so that Divine connection can be experienced.

It is believed that there are certain times of the day when your meditation will be more potent, for instance some say midday. Do what suits you best, your meditation time may be at sunrise or sunset, after lunch or before bedtime.

Also bear in mind powerful dates, for example 9/9/2009 or the 7th day of the 7th month (see chapter on numerology).

Start by keeping it simple and basically the three main techniques to try are:

1) Focus on the breath
2) Use visualizations
3) Use sound - chanting, music, drum, bells etc

Focusing on the Breath

Use the breath as your point of focus.

Simply observe your breathing.

Feel what is happening in the body and take your focus to where you feel the prana going.

Note things like the natural pauses after you inhale and after you exhale.

Watch the breath settle.

Even focusing on this simple method will lead you into a meditative state and will help you to relax and quieten your mind.

Extending the Exhale

As you focus on your breath, count the inhale and then count the exhale. Try to make the exhale longer than the inhale. For example, inhale for the count of 5, exhale for the count of 10.

Using the Breath with a Visualization

Focus on an external object while observing the breath.

Visualize yourself standing on a beach. Focus on your breathing.

Observe your inhale, pause. Observe your exhale, pause.

As you inhale see the wave coming in to the shore, pause.

As you exhale, see the wave going back out to the sea, pause.

Repeat several times.

Bring yourself back by focusing on just the breath, feel the abdomen rising on the inhale, falling on the exhale.

Vipassana Meditation

This is also known as 'Insight Meditation'.

This form of Meditation is for stilling the mind, to stop the activity of the mind, to bring peace. The idea is that once you have achieved this stillness, you will then have insights and self realizations. Vipassana Meditation takes you out of your everyday rational mind.

As usual, find a comfortable position, preferably seated.

Take your time to settle. Take your focus to your abdomen.

29

Observe and feel the abdomen rising as you inhale. Observe and feel the abdomen falling as you exhale. Repeat the mantra in your head; 'rising' on the inhale, 'falling' on the exhale. Repeat this mantra over and over in your mind.

If thoughts come into your mind, repeat the mantra 'thinking, thinking, thinking,' over and over, until the thoughts go away.

If you have an itch, (it is common to get an itchy nose for instance, or feel a tickle on your face when meditating), repeat the mantra 'itching, itching, itching' until it goes away.

Go back to the mantra of 'rising' on the inhale and 'falling' on the exhale.

If your back starts to ache, repeat the mantra 'pain, pain, pain' until it goes away. Return to the mantra of 'rising' on the inhale, 'falling' on the exhale.

By practicing this simple form of Meditation regularly, you will become deeply relaxed, your mind will be quiet and in time you will go into the next stage of meditation, becoming fully focused on the mantras.

Meditating on a Higher Energy
As before, sit comfortably and take time to relax..

Focus on the breath.

Take your focus outside your body.

Take your focus several feet away from your body.

Take your focus a hundred feet away from your body.

Take your focus as far away as you wish.

Ask - 'What is this Higher Energy?'

See what comes.

(Examples are Pure Energy, Light, The Great Spirit, The Great Divine, God, or it could be the Ocean or The Sky.)

Mindful Meditation
Like the above, in this form of meditation, you are not actively looking for visions and do not have an agenda as such. Simply

start to quiet the mind by focusing on the breath, for instance. If any thoughts come into your mind, don't chat back, in other words don't respond to the thought. The thought will eventually leave. If you react, then you will end up chatting away in your head. Just be in the present which is sitting meditating and being in a peaceful place, not the past, not the future. Let the mind settle.

Using Visualizations in Meditation

With the breath being one method of Meditation, Visualizations are another. If you have an active imagination, then this method could be for you.

Visualizations in Meditation involve focusing on an object which could be in the form of a flower, something in nature like a forest, sitting on top of a mountain, or being out in an open space in the countryside. I would suggest to start with to keep it simple and try focusing on a picture of say a beautiful flower, or a picture of an enlightened person. Focusing on the flame of a candle is another example. Another way is to use a statue of Buddha which emanates peace and healing.

Start by simply staring at this object and then after a while shut your eyes and then try and see the image in your mind and just focus at that point.

Gradually extend your concentration over a period of time. For instance visualize yourself on top of a mountain. Really let your imagination take you to this sacred place. In your mind start to see yourself there, feel the vast open space, breathe the fresh air.

If you like being near water, try visualizing yourself walking along a beach, and again start to see the ocean, feel the sand underneath your feet, maybe walk in the water. See dolphins playing in the sea.

If you like nature, visualize yourself walking in a forest, see wildlife around you, see the beautiful trees and plants, really connect to everything around you.

A Visualization Meditation using the Breath as a Focus with Visualization

Sit comfortably, either on the floor using a block or cushion for support if you wish, or on a chair, ideally with your feet on the floor.

Close your eyes.

Bring your focus to your chest and throat area.

Focus on the breath. The inhale, the exhale. Acknowledge the natural pause after the inhale. Acknowledge the natural pause after the exhale. Observe this rhythm - four parts to the breath - inhale - pause - exhale - pause.

Now find yourself walking along a beach - a long stretch of sandy beach, you are all alone. The sun is shining. To your left is the ocean and to your right are cliffs and rocks. You walk along the beach and feel the warmth of the sand under your feet. With each step you take, you are mindful. The sky is a beautiful blue color. The sun is shining down on you providing you with warmth, energy and light. This makes you feel warm, energized and full of light.

You stop and you look at the sea - a beautiful turquoise color.

You take in the vastness of the ocean. Breathing in the fresh air.

Observing the waves coming in to the shore and going back out to the ocean.

As the waves come in towards the shore, focus on your inhale.

Feel the inhale lengthening.

As the waves go back out, focus on your exhale.

Feel the exhale lengthening.

Keep repeating this in your mind - inhale - the waves come in - pause. Exhale - the waves go back out taking everything away - pause.

Feel as if you are these waves.

Feel part of the ocean.

Feel the space.

Take some time being mindful in this space.

Now it is time to walk back along the beach where you came from.

The ocean is now on your right and the cliffs and rocks are on your left.

Take a slow walk back, feeling the sand underneath your feet.

Take your attention to your chest and throat area, focus on your breathing. Feel yourself breathing - feel the chest rising on the inhale, feel the ribcage expanding out to the side. On the exhale feel the chest slightly falling, the ribcage coming back in.

Hear your breath.

Slowly bring your awareness back. Feel your feet on the floor, feel the ground beneath you. See roots coming out of your feet into Mother Earth.

Visualize yourself in a grounding spiral of white light covering the top of your head down to your feet.

Start to move your fingers and toes.

Open your eyes.

Take a nice deep breath.

Take a gentle stretch.

Visualization using the Elements

Within each of us are the four elements of earth, air, water and fire plus the spiritual element of ether.

You can get in tune with the self by focusing on these elements:

Visualize yourself walking along a sandy beach. Feel the sand coming up between your toes. The sun is shining down upon you. Stop and lie down on the sand. Feel the energy of the sun - Fire. How does it feel?

You get up from the sand and look at the ocean. It is still, like a pond. Step into the water and feel the coolness over your feet.

The water is crystal clear. How do you feel connecting to the element of water?

You go back onto the beach and turn around and ahead of you is a path. Go to the path and walk slowly up it. The path takes you up a hill and ahead of you is a gate. Go through the gate and enter a landscape of beautiful lush green countryside. There are trees, wild flowers and wild animals. Feel the connection to Mother Earth with every step you take. How does it feel to be connected to the element of earth?

You feel a cool breeze and look up and see the trees swaying. You are alone in this beautiful landscape. You breathe in, the fresh air filling your lungs, taking long, slow, deep breaths. Feel the connection of the element of air. How does it feel?

You look up to the sky. It is a beautiful pale blue. Breath in this vast open space. Feel yourself being taken up to the clouds. Feel ether. How does it feel?

Slowly bring yourself back to the present,

Ground yourself to finish.

Focusing on the Self

Try focusing within the Self. For instance take your attention to one place within the body. An example could be just focusing on the heart space, or the brow area or the hollow below the throat. Maybe focusing on one Chakra at a time. You will feel the whole body relaxing and you will become very still and quiet.

Chakra Cleansing Meditation

This is a very healing Meditation where you take your focus to one Chakra at a time and call in healing energies from The Great Divine. If done patiently, this Meditation should take around 20 minutes to half an hour.

Get yourself in a comfortable sitting position. Feel grounded before you start. Ask The Great Divine to send you healing energies. Take your focus to your Crown Chakra. See the color white. Hold your focus at the top of your head and see this white light cleansing and healing this energy center. Feel the connection to The Great Divine. Stay here until you feel ready to move on.

Take your focus to your Brow Chakra. See the color purple. See this purple energy cleansing and healing your brow energy center. Bring peace to your mind. Stay here until you feel it is right to move on.

Take your focus to your Throat Chakra. See a blue light. See this blue energy healing and cleansing your throat area taking away any tension you may have in your neck and shoulders. Move on when you feel it is right.

Take your focus to your Heart Chakra. See the color pink and visualize this beautiful healing pink light cleansing your heart area. Let go of old emotions. Allow yourself to feel love. Stay here until you feel ready to move on.

Take your focus to your Solar Plexus Chakra. See a bright yellow light and allow this light to cleanse and heal your energy center around your stomach area. Your digestion will be calmed. Feel energized. Stay here until you feel ready to move on.

Take your focus to your Sacral Chakra, below the navel. See a beautiful orange light and allow this healing light to cleanse your Sacral energy center. Let go of deep emotions from the past. Move on when you feel ready.

Now take your focus to the Base Chakra, the very base of the spine. See a beautiful earthy red healing light. Allow this healing light to cleanse and heal your Base energy center. Feel connected to Mother Earth, feel grounded.

Finish by seeing roots coming out of your feet into Mother Earth.

Mantra Meditation
A mantra is a sacred sound. A Mantra could be one word like 'Om' or many words like 'Om mani padme hum', which is the

Buddhist mantra of compassion. By repeating a mantra your mind will become engaged.

Affirmations are positive words to use as the object of focus for Meditation. You repeat the saying in your mind several times. Examples of an affirmation could be:

'Today I am happy and at peace'
'I feel energized and healed'
'My self-esteem is high and I love myself'
'My thoughts are positive'
'I ask for healing to be sent to myself and out to the Planet'

Using Meditation to Solve an Issue

If you are at a crossroads in your life and need guidance then meditate on the issue in your life and ask The Great Divine for help. Then be patient and see what comes to your mind.

Walking Meditation

Stand in the Mountain Posture - feet hip width apart, knees soft, hips slightly tucked under, chest open, shoulders back, chin slightly tucked back to lengthen the neck.

Feel your feet firmly on the ground, feel connected to Mother Earth. Feel as if your head is in the sky. Take a while to settle, focusing the mind. Step forward with the right foot and place the heel on the ground. Repeat the mantra 'Right goes forth' either in your mind or out loud and place the rest of the right foot on the ground. Step forward with the left foot and place the heel on the ground. Repeat the mantra 'Left goes forth' and place the rest of the left foot on the ground. Repeat, walking round the room or garden, or up and down. Repeat many times being mindful and really taking your time, almost as if you are in slow motion.

Levels of Meditation

You will experience different levels of Meditation if you practice regularly. Concentration is the level at the beginning. You use an object to focus on whether this object is the breath, a visualization or a mantra. Your mind at times will wander off to everyday thoughts such as filling the car up with fuel, going shopping, or what you are having for dinner.

The more you practice, the easier you will find it to take your Meditation to the next level which is where your mind will stay focused for some length of time. There are no distractions, your mind is still without trying to take you to the past, or to the future.

The next level which is known as 'Samadhi' is where you can stay in a meditative state for a sustained amount of time. Nothing distracts you, nothing exists, there is no sense of time, only timelessness.

Benefits of Meditation

By practicing regular Meditation you will start to feel the benefits. By becoming relaxed your physical body, your mind, your emotions and spirit will be in a balanced and healthy state. The physical benefits are many and include a relaxed nervous system, and a balanced endocrine system. By balancing the hormones you will feel so much better especially when the hormones are out of kilter at times for women like during menstruation and during the menopause.

The benefits for the mind are that Meditation will bring peace to the mind, which will calm the mental energy. This will calm the activity that can drive you insane with that annoying voice always controlling you. Mental peace will keep away headaches and tension.

The benefits for the emotions of bringing harmony will also result in a healthy body as it is believed that physical ailments often are a result of imbalanced emotions.

(A healthy mind will result in a healthy body.)

Finding a Meditation Group

If, like most people, you find meditating difficult and frustrating, try joining a group. Use your discernment and you will benefit enormously from finding the right teacher. You will see meditation classes as part of Yoga classes and at various centers connected to Buddhism, Healing centers and Complementary Health Centers. These groups tend to be large and although they hold great value, will not be as beneficial as smaller, more personal groups. You may be lucky and find someone who takes small groups in their own homes. These tend to be more in-depth and beneficial.

Finding the right teacher

It is often said that when the time is right, the right teacher comes along. This seems to be so true. Put it out to The Divine that you are seeking a Teacher to help you on your spiritual path. A good teacher will not be in ego, so if they talk about how successful they are and how good they are, then perhaps look elsewhere. If they try to impress you by tales of channelling Jesus Christ or other Ascended Masters then beware that their ego could be inflated. A good teacher will often channel from a high energy and may not know who they are working with or may know but choose not to disclose such information. With regards to costs, ask yourself after the session how you feel. Was the cost right to you, was it too much, too little so that you didn't feel you were in a professional environment, etc. A good teacher will empower you. If you feel you are looking up to your teacher like a Guru, then the energy is not right for you. If you idolize your teacher, you will be giving your power away and that is not healthy for either of you.

After your meditation class, you should feel a sense of peace and healing. You should sleep well and feel the benefits for days after. The only disadvantage of smaller groups is that although personal feedback takes place, which can be very healing, this can lead into a therapy session which is not the idea, but a good teacher will be able to see this.

You should like the energy of your Teacher and follow your instincts.

The purpose of spiritual knowledge is the awakening of the soul and the transformational experience. In the Far East it is believed that in order to be effective, spiritual knowledge must be transmitted from one human being to another, from teacher to disciple. To a certain extent this is true, a good teacher will empower you and inspire you and will light the candle within you if you liken this to your Soul. Books will give you lots of information but cannot give you wisdom. It is knowing when you need a teacher and when you need to be The Hermit and take some time on your own.

To Lead a Meditation
To lead a group in meditation should not really be taken on by beginners. This would be for the more advanced who have been practicing regular meditation, who have very grounded energies but also who are in union with their Spirit Guides and Masters. You will know yourself when you are ready and you will be inspired.

Preparation
Create a sacred space by clearing the energy, smudging, lighting a candle or lighting incense (be aware that some people have allergies to incense). Ask for protection from your Spirit Guides, ask to be grounded and connected and to work for the highest good of your group.

Meditate before everyone arrives and ask your Guides to channel an appropriate meditation. (The channelled meditations are always extremely healing and powerful and are so much better that meditations read straight from books or from the internet).

Make sure your room is at the right temperature - not too warm, not too cold. I generally find that once your group arrives and the energies start to rise, the room generally gets warmer.

Make sure everyone is comfortable.

Decide whether you will be using background music.

Ask everyone to close their eyes.

Channel

Take a few minutes to relax your group which means a good 5-8 minutes. Assess your group. They may need a bit longer, especially more for beginners and less for those who are more practiced.

Again, ask your Guides to now channel an appropriate meditation.

Although you are channelling, you will need to occasionally check around the group - someone may be crying and might need tissues for instance, or comforting and healing, and you will need to try to make sure the rest of the group is not disturbed.

When the meditation is complete, bring the group back really slowly which means bringing the awareness back into the body, grounding the energies by, say, seeing roots coming out of the feet into the earth, feeling yourself sitting on the chair or lying, moving the fingers and the toes, taking a deep breath and opening the eyes when they are ready.

I sometimes sound the Tibetan bells really lightly or use the Tibetan Singing Bowl.

Check around the room to make sure everyone is back.

Chapter 4

Energy Healing

Reiki

Energy Healing techniques such as Reiki have helped to spread the word around the world of healing the body by channeling energy from Spirit, through the Channeler, the Healer, into the Healee, the recipient. This Divine energy is channeled through the hands of the Healer into the recipient. This energy will go where it is needed. It is not the Healer doing the healing, they are the Channeler, it is the Divine Energy. This Divine Energy will help to clear blockages of energy in the body at a physical level, a mental level and an emotional level. This healing will take place at a soul level over a period of time, as long as the Healee is doing some form of spiritual practice mentioned previously which means Physical energy work such as Yoga, working with the breath, meditation and connecting to the Soul through active self-study and awareness. In other words receiving Reiki regularly will of course benefit you but there is more active work to do to become free from wounds completely.

This form of healing works at a spiritual level.

The intention to want to help the Self and others in the purest form is all that is required to become a Healer. Everyone can heal as long as they have the right intent and can let go of ego.

To become a Reiki Healer you will need to be attuned by a Reiki Master who has themself received attunements. These attunements on the whole come in three levels - Reiki I, Reiki II and Reiki III. By receiving an attunement your upper Chakras will be opened up and your connection with The Great Divine will become closer. Your lower Chakras should be connected to Mother Earth and you will ground your energies by becoming closer to nature and literally feeling the earth beneath you. There is a danger of becoming too attached to the upper spiritual energies and neglecting the earthing grounding energies, and this must be avoided. Reiki attunements will open you up to receive the beautiful healing energies of The Great Divine.

Reiki was made known by Dr Usui, from Japan, in the late nineteenth century on his travels. He discovered Sanskrit text which was later revealed as ancient healing symbols. He went up a mountain and meditated for 21 days on these symbols and received great realizations during this period.

He passed on his knowledge by attuning others who then went on to attune further people. There are various forms of Reiki but the essence is the same, rather like Buddhism.

After your attunement you should follow a 21 day cleansing period as Dr Usui did when he spent 21 days up the mountain eating and drinking very little.

Reiki Treatment

A Reiki healing treatment should last around 45 minutes to one hour. You should lie down on a healing couch/treatment couch and the Practitioner will lay their hands either on your physical body or in your aura. (It is also possible to receive Reiki sitting in a chair). They will commune with the Healing Master of Reiki, Dr Usui, plus healing Guides and Helpers in Spirit. Healing energy will then be channeled through the hands of the Practitioner and the Healee may feel warmth, tingling or possibly cool air. They may not feel anything at all. This is a deeply relaxing treatment and should be a very positive and beautiful experience.

The Practitioner usually starts at the head and works their way down the body to the feet. You will then turn over on the couch and the Practitioner will work down the back of your body finishing at your feet. Finishing at the feet is very grounding and will help to bring your awareness back to the present.

Modules for Reiki Courses
Reiki I Attunement

You will be attuned to the Reiki healing energy by a Reiki Master who will draw the sacred symbols in your aura over parts of your body such as your Crown Chakra, your Brow Chakra, your hands and your feet.

~ Reiki I is about learning how to self heal and after the 21 day cleansing period, how to heal family and friends.

In Reiki I, you should cover the following:

The history of Reiki.

The energy system and chakras in detail.

How to ground and protect yourself when working with energy.

Who, what and when to use Reiki.

An explanation of the 21 day cleansing process. After receiving an attunement to open you up to the healing energy, you should follow a 21 day cleansing period. This should be treated like a detoxification period which means abstaining from alcohol, caffeine, red meat, sugar and dairy products. You should drink plenty of water and try to eat organic fruit and vegetables.

You will spend three days meditating on each chakra, starting at the Base Chakra, working your way up the centers until by the 21st day, you finish at the Crown chakra.

You should cover the following practical work:

The attunement by The Reiki Master

The method to cleanse each chakra.

How to self-heal.

How to do a 10 minute healing on someone else who is seated.

Full Reiki hand positions - how to do a full treatment on another.

Reiki II Attunement

~ There should be a minimum of 3 months between Reiki I and Reiki II. This is to allow your own healing process to take place. You may need much longer.

~ Reiki II is for those who wish to heal others and must display the intent to heal.

~ Reiki II should be a minimum of two days.

In Reiki II you should cover the following:

Discuss the 21 day cleansing period as before.

Symbols and mantras - meanings and uses. For using on the Self and others. These sacred symbols carry healing energy and the name of the symbol (Mantra) is repeated three times.

Distant healing - healing energy can be sent to those in need wherever they are on the Planet.

Reiki lineage - you will learn who attuned your Teacher, then who attuned your Teacher's Teacher and so on.

Contraindications - Reiki is safe for most, except for those who have severe mental health problems. It is wise to leave it to the professional therapists to deal with people whom you may be unsure about and unqualified to deal with them and their reaction. (Surfacing old wounds and issues may bring up anger and rage for instance). Energy healing can bring emotions to the surface and often tears come. Other times a pure relaxation and blissful state occurs.

In Reiki II you will cover the following practical work:

Attunement to the second degree.

How to use symbols on the self and others.

Distant healing.

Joshin Kokyuu-Ho (Reiki meditation). Inhaling pure Reiki healing energy into your body and taking this energy into the Base Chakra and then exhaling any impurities and tension.

Cleansing each chakra.

Full Reiki hand positions with symbols.

Reiki III

~ You must hold Reiki I and Reiki II certificates.
~ You must wait a minimum of two years and have actively been treating clients.
~ You must display the intent to heal with compassion and be emotionally ready.
~ It is a two day, 16 hour course.

The following theory should be covered in Reiki III
Revision of the above.
A discussion of the 21 day cleansing period.
The Master symbols.
By this stage Practitioners should be quite in tune with their own wounds and should have continued to work on their own self-development.
Pet healing - pets respond really well to the healing energies of Reiki.
Working intuitively.

Reiki Master Teacher Training Course

~ For students who have the above certificates and are ready to attune others.
~ They must display the intent to heal and teach with compassion and be emotionally ready.

The following should be covered:
Discuss in detail the responsibility of the course, which means the responsibility of working with others at an energy level and support. Not taking on others' problems. Learning to be compassionate and have good listening skills. Realizing that you cannot solve and heal everyone else, they have to take on that responsibility themselves.
To discuss any issues and experiences to-date.
How to attune students.

Reiki Masters should continue to work on their own wounds and self-development.

Spiritual healing in all the different forms and names can bring up emotions and past traumas not only in this life, but past lives. Therefore the Healer should feel ready to take on this responsibility and be prepared for this.

Summary

Now there are many different names and techniques for therapies in the form of spiritual healing. There are many different lengths of time for training. Basically the energy is that of the Great Divine. Beware of those who are in ego and are out to earn themselves praise and wealth. They are not sincere or clear channels even though they will put that idea out to those who will listen.

With experience and practice, the Healer will know exactly where to place the hands on the body, and hand positions and the sequence they have been taught by their teacher will not be necessary, since they are now working with their intuition. Once the hands are placed on the body, the energy will go where it is needed and the Healer does not need to assess, know or diagnose anything, just simply to place the hands on the Healee, letting go of any ego.

Reiki and these healing techniques are for all at all times which means you do not have to wait until you are unwell before you go for healing. We all, as humans, have blocked energy. It is wonderful for those recovering from an illness or operation.

It is also a beautiful thing to receive Reiki at the end of life, to help you pass to the Spirit World.

The clearer the Healer is as a channel the more powerful the healing, which means the Reiki Practitioner needs to do continuous chakra cleansing, needs to receive healing, to study sacred texts and self study.

Healing with Color

Spirit Guides often communicate with color and in my own experience this means the following:

White

White is pure light and love. When white is seen around the crown chakra, it would mean a good connection with Spirit. Angels often communicate with a white light.

Purple

Purple is a strong healing color and when I see purple, I sense the presence of Angels. The healing energy is very powerful. It is a very spiritual color and can often indicate that the healee has healing abilities. On a physical level, it indicates that hormonal issues could be going on. It also suggests that there are psychic abilities.

Blue

Blue is another strong healing color and for me, it would indicate possible issues around the neck area which could be physical in the form of tension across the neck and shoulders or possibly thyroid issues. It may also indicate communication blockages.

Turquoise

This color indicates someone who can accept divine love and give a 'heartful' of love.

Green

Green is another healing color which will be seen when Angels are present. It has a beautiful calm energy and indicates healing around the heart chakra.

Yellow

This bright color represents the solar plexus chakra and can indicate a bright and confident person with a 'sunny' outlook on life. When seen in the aura around the stomach area this would indicate possible issues with the digestive system.

Orange

Orange indicates balance and harmony. When seen in the aura around the sacral chakra this would mean possibly emotional blockages and childhood issues.

Red

Red indicates passion and anger. If the red is bright around the base chakra it would indicate someone is grounded. If the red is a brown color, it would indicate being too grounded with over-materialistic thoughts, neglecting spirituality and thoughts about the physical body.

Black

I often see a shade of dark gray or black when blockages are present in the physical body. These blockages are simply that - blocked energy. Sometimes it may have manifested into a physical pain or illness.

Gray

Gray would indicate someone with clouded thoughts. It rej re-sents someone whose energy is low. Their thoughts would predominately be dark, depressing with no clarity.

Gold

Gold would represent someone who is working at a very high vibration. It would indicate a whole Soul, someone who has done much work on clearing their chakras.

Pink

Pink along with green are the colors of the heart chakra. Pink represents love and the ability to love unconditionally. When Gold and pink are seen together, Angels and Healing Guides are present.

When you commune with your own Guides, you will have your own meanings of color energy.

Chapter 5

Sacred Texts

Patanjali's Yoga Sutras as a sacred text
Introduction

Patanjali's Yoga Sutras are an example of a sacred text. These Sutras are the foundation of the real knowledge and they make sense, having a clear message. There are various translations, and one which is particularly relevant to the modern aspirant is *Your Quest for a Spiritual Life* published by O-Books, written by myself.

Patanjali was a Sage believed to be around over two and a half thousand years ago. He wrote these Sutras in Sanskrit, an ancient Indo-European language. If everyone studied these words and took something from them, the world would be a better place, more in harmony and balance.

Sutra means thread and Patanjali wrote these words in the form of aphorisms, each one interwoven into the next.

The Sutras are in four chapters with each chapter varying from around 40-50 aphorisms.

Chapter 1 - Samadhi Pada - Concentration

The first chapter is Samadhi Pada which examines the art of concentration, and teaches how to focus and meditate. The mind is very hard to train and control and this chapter discusses the mind; how busy it is and the distractions it faces. How our mind can be both our friend and our enemy, how it can be heavy, sending out negative thoughts and sometimes even depressive thoughts. How the mind can be energetic with thoughts racing around in our heads or in the light state - where the mind can be calm and serene.

The goal is Samadhi. This state of consciousness is a state that we experience in meditation - a blissful, peaceful, enlightened state. To reach that goal, we must practice regularly and work on healing the self. The sutras also mention that although Samadhi is the goal, once reached, the work is not all done. Don't take a step back and think that is it, the spiritual path carries on and we never stop learning. Once Samadhi has been attained the higher truth can be revealed.

These wisdoms remind us to have awareness, to be in the present.

The Mind

The mind, especially in these days of constant hustle, is very active. Years ago spiritual seekers would have spent time alone for contemplation and to find enlightenment through meditation and this would have been for years and years of their life, if not their whole life.

In modern times, we do not have this luxury of having total solitude to find our peace, we have to fit it into our daily lives of work and family. So our minds are full of stress, worries about money for the rent or mortgage, buying groceries, going to work and meeting the challenges that brings to us, children, family, worrying how we look, etc. What an overload of mental energy!

By practicing Yoga, Breathing techniques and Meditation, you will gain peace of mind and this will liberate you from the mind's activities. Daily life will then be easier to cope with as you will feel more balanced and in harmony.

Chapter one explains the art of concentration which eventually brings meditation. This calms the mind of its constant activity, and you can then be in touch with your true self - your soul.

A state known as Samadhi is attainable and allows total concentration and focus in your meditative state which can be maintained for a period of time rather than the mind flickering in and out. The mind will then be at peace and in total stillness.

This is stillness from everyday thoughts and this stillness can make you open to impressions or intuitions from a higher plane.

If you pray and / or meditate, the question is asked 'With whom are you communing?' You may gain an understanding of your own beliefs or feel a connection to God, Buddha, an Icon or The Great Divine. It is certainly an energy greater than yourself. This will lead you to your own belief system rather than having your parents' beliefs, so this may or may not be different from your cultural upbringing.

You may believe that your God is a separate energy which means duality, or you may believe that you have God within, which means non-duality.

Grounding is an important issue. When you start to seek spiritually it is important to have your feet firmly on the ground before connecting to higher energies which means literally staying still, feeling the energies of the earth, being connected. The lower three chakras are the grounding energies within.

Different techniques of meditation are discussed, such as focusing on a Mantra such as Om, focusing on an object such as a statue of Buddha or a picture of an enlightened sage such as Sri Swami Sivananda. Other objects to focus on could be a part of the body such as the heart or the chakras.

By stilling the mind, the true self can be revealed and therefore wisdom which has been locked up inside shines through. Insights and self-realizations will be experienced as you become more connected to the higher truths.

Chapter one finishes by stating that life is about cycles which means while you may have completed a cycle, met your challenges and lessons, there is more work to do to enable you to reach a higher enlightened state.

Chapter 2 of Patanjali's Yoga Sutras - Sadhana Pada -

Practice and Discipline

Now you have an understanding of how the mind works and how it can distract you. This is the chapter on practices. We are told how to practice through discipline, study and dedication to an ideal, i.e.: an energy greater than ourselves. We learn about our obstacles to growth and how we can overcome them. This chapter talks about Kriya Yoga - self discipline is required for you to practice Yoga on a regular basis. You have to keep putting more energy in and like anything else, you will get more back.

Karma is mentioned in chapter 2 - how your past actions can affect you later on. How we are responsible for every action, deed and thought - for as we sow, so shall we reap.

The kleshas are brought to your awareness here - the obstacles to your spiritual path, how ignorance blocks our view.

Patanjali's eight limbs of Yoga are discussed, which gives insight on your outlook to others as well as your attitude towards yourself. This explains the different steps of growth.

The third, fourth and fifth limbs of Astanga Yoga are explained - Asana (postures), Pranayama (breathing) and Pratyahara (going inwards) and how the breath work is really important to practice.

We learn in this chapter that the search is within the self. It is like discovering a golden key - to unlock the wisdom.

Kriya Yoga

Kriya Yoga is composed of three actions which are self discipline, self-study and surrender to the Great Divine.

Self discipline is required in order for you to practice daily your energy movement (maybe Yoga postures), breathing techniques and meditation. You may reach a level of your spiritual practice where you start to feel the benefits such as Self-realizations, peace in the mind, harmony and balance. This doesn't mean to say that you have reached enlightenment and liberation, there is more work to do. You should recognize how far you have come on your quest and acknowledge that discipline and regular practice is required in order for you to progress and evolve spiritually.

Self-study

This means studying the self, finding out how others see you, how you react to others and looking at your own wounds. Another way to study the self is through the practice of Meditation and the more you practice, the more self-realizations will come. It also comes from studying sacred texts such as The Yoga Sutras.

A good start is to look at your birth chart. From your date of birth you will discover your sun sign, your moon sign and your ascendant sign. You will find out what elements you are particularly working with which means earth, air, fire and water. (See also the Chapter on Numerology to find out your destiny number and the challenges you are likely to meet).

Earth energies are very physical and grounding and often too much of this energy can result in being too grounded, not being in touch with the spiritual self or being too materialistic - placing too much desire and attachment to material items such as money, house, car, etc. Too little earth energy could result in being the opposite; ungrounded with your head in the clouds, no interest in work, money, home etc; being in a fantasy world. A good balance of energies will mean harmony between the spiritual world and the material world.

Air energies are the opposite of earth. Whereas earth is grounding, air relates to your mental energy; your mind. Too much air energy will result in an overactive mind, someone who is ungrounded, 'away with the Faeries', in a 'little world of their own' out of touch with reality. Too little will result in a dull, heavy mind or someone whose energies stay too grounded, out of touch with the spiritual self. A good balance of air energy will mean someone who can still the mind, be in touch with the world of material energies such as work, family, money but also be in touch with their spiritual self.

Fire energies are all about spirit; spirit to take action and go forward in life. Too much fire energy will result in having a 'gung-ho' approach - not thinking, just rushing ahead taking action. Too much fire and you will get burned. Too little fire energy will result in lethargy, tiredness, no ambition, no confidence to move forward in life, being 'stuck in a rut'. A good balance of fire energy will be someone who can control their actions, ideas and ambitions in a positive way and channel their creativity in the right direction.

Water energies are connected to our emotions. Too much water will make you over-emotional, needy, unable to control your emotions and power. (Look at the damage the Tsunami did). Too little will result in not being in touch with your emotions, not being able to express your feelings. A good balance of water energy would be someone who understands their own emotions, is in touch with their feelings and can express their emotions when needed in the right way which means saying what is needed to be said in a situation without letting the emotions get out of hand.

The Astrological signs and their related elements:

Aires - fire

Taurus - earth

Gemini - air

Cancer - water

Leo - fire

Virgo - earth

Libra - air

Scorpio - water

Sagittarius - fire

Capricorn - earth

Aquarius - air

Pisces - water

By studying your own energies you will probably start to look at those people around you; your partner, family andfriends, and you will not only find out more about yourself but also start to understand others and this will help in relationships.

Shamanic Chant
Earth my body
Water my blood
Air my breath
And
Fire my spirit

The five afflictions
The obstacles to your spiritual path are know as the five afflictions. These are:

Spiritual ignorance
Ego
Desire and attachment
Hatred and anger
Fear

Spiritual Ignorance
Spiritual ignorance is the root of the problem and is the basis of the other four.

Most people go through life unaware of their spiritual paths. Some might say they are 'blissfully ignorant' as once you start self-study your own wounds will surface. While these wounds are processed and transformation takes place through active awareness, it can be difficult at times. Unaware people may never find true peace and happiness. Spiritual ignorance will only suppress wounds. A period of healing can bring pain as the wounds heal, but it will be followed by joy and pleasure as you feel like a 'heavy weight' has been lifted from your shoulders.

Ego

Egoism is pride, the 'I am'.

The Soul is the seer - pure spirit consciousness. The ego sits in the mind. The ego can be seen as an obstacle to your true self, as it takes it upon itself to try to connect to the soul, as it sees itself as the seer. The true seer is the soul.

The mind is not the true self, the Soul - the seer is the true self.

The ego is seen as a Male energy - Sun energy. Too little of this energy may result in low self-esteem and low confidence, and too much of this energy may result in an inflated opinion of the self; overly confident and selfish.

It takes much experience to understand whether ego is leading you or whether it is your intuition - your deep voice of knowing. The ego tries very hard to control us but in fact the Sutras talk about renunciation of the ego - letting go, being in control rather than letting the ego lead.

Desire and Attachment

The next obstacle is in the form of desire and attachment.

It is very easy to become attached to pleasure and happiness. You may think an object will satisfy your desire or make you happy. It could do initially, but in time there will be consequences. For example, if you desire a new car when the car you already have is quite functional and reliable and fits your needs, and you go out and purchase this new car (pleasure) with a three year financial loan because you have not got the cash for it, you may then spend the next three years struggling (pain) to pay for the loan on a car that you didn't really need in the first place.

Another example is the desire for a piece of cake full of sugar and cream (pleasure). Deep down you know that the piece of cake won't be good for your troubled digestive system but you eat it anyway. Later on you suffer indigestion, the pain from satisfying a desire.

Attachment to a desire is wanting something that perhaps you have previously experienced which brought you pleasure, but is not necessarily something you actually need.

When your mind is full of desires, you are practicing attachment. The Sutras often mention renunciation of attachments.

Hatred and Anger

The next obstacle is in the form of anger and hatred.

The mind can become attached to those things which bring us sorrow and pain - such as unfulfilled desires, hatred to others or the Self, dwelling on wounds. This will lead to being self-absorbed, being the victim, and will block your spiritual growth.

Once in this painful state it is like a spiral going down and down, and it is then a huge challenge to come up again.

Fear

Fear is the next obstacle, for example fear of death.

Fears are blocks to our paths. The only way to overcome fears is to face them and deal with them. A fear of the dark is a common fear but it is often just in the imagination. Another example is fear of spiders and again this is the imagination working overtime as often spiders cannot actually harm us, especially in Great Britain.

Most people have a fear of dying. Death of the physical body is not death of the Soul - it is going home to the spirit world. Upon death, as the very last exhale is taken, the soul will leave the physical body and pass over into the world of spirit - The Great Divine Consciousness.

When in a true Yogic state it is possible to feel the Spirit within connecting to the Great Spirit around, then all fears will be lost.

All of these afflictions are subtle and are not obvious unless self-study is practiced.

Meditation and reflection will help to heal the afflictions.

Contemplation and reflection are needed and can be achieved through prayer, meditation or discussion with a Wise Sage or Therapist / Healer. Sometimes others can see what you cannot see for yourself.

By working on the Soul, healing wounds from this life and attachments to past lives, the spirit can be free.

You will be here in this life with certain lessons and challenges. Understand what you are here to do. (Numerology is a great help for this).

Karma

Before you incarnated into this life, your soul will have chosen what circumstances to be born into; your family, surroundings, environment. Through your ancestors, your bloodline will bring you gifts and freedoms and also limitations and burdens. This is seen as family karma. This will give you the necessary learning for your Soul to evolve.

You will be born with individual karma, actions from past lives that have generated karma that could be good or bad or a mixture of both.

You can study your family karma by observing your family patterns, behaviors; the gifts and freedoms your parents give you as well as the burdens and limitations. So much can be discovered.

You will have imprints from this life as well as imprints from past lives. These imprints are the seeds you have sown; your past actions. You may not be aware of these past actions but they are imprinted in your sub-conscious. If you chose to work on this, then certain Therapists may help but be aware that it is the Soul seeking this, not the ego. Going into past lives can be very painful, and can be damaging to the mind if the environment is not right or adequate support is not available. It is thought by

59

some that regressing into past lives can help with healing and shifting wounds and patterns that you carry in this life. Often when working at a deep level images of past lives can appear anyway. If this happens attachments should not be made.

Past actions bear fruit and depending on what the action was, good or bad, will decide whether the fruit bears pleasure or pain.

Once you have recognized bad actions and thoughts, then already the Karma is starting to release. Being aware is the key. Don't think that because you made a mistake in the past, you are going to pay for it with pain now. Recognize your mistake and genuinely learn from the lesson.

Negative thought waves filter out into the Universe. Be aware of your thoughts. If you think something harsh about someone, try to correct yourself and send out positive thoughts.

Energy follows thought.

The Eight Limbs of Yoga

The eight limbs are the structural framework of Yoga practice and they are known as 'Astanga Yoga'. Often it is thought that Astanga Yoga is the strong physical Yoga but the true meaning of Astanga is the following:

1) Yama

Yama means 'code of conduct' and there are five Yamas. These are non-violence, not harming any living being; truth, speaking your truths and expressing what you feel needs to be said without harming others with your words; not stealing or taking from others what is not yours; moderation; and not being greedy.

2) Niyama

Niyamas are disciplines for the self, and there are five. These are cleanliness, which applies to the mental body with purity of thoughts and cleanliness of the mind and also the physical body which should be kept cleaned with a daily cleansing routine and also purity of the body in the form of eating and drinking healthily; being content with what you have and not continually desiring material objects or what other people possess; having self-discipline to take your daily practice or Yoga; self-study; and surrendering to The Great Divine.

3) Asana

Asana means 'postures' and it is through posture work that most people come into Yoga, especially in the West. These postures will shift energy in the body and toxins will be released. This is often subtle, but at the same time very powerful. Posture work should be performed with comfort as well as alertness. It is a myth that Yoga is about stretching a leg behind your head, but more realistically the postures are actually effective ways of shifting energy and stretching the muscles as well as keeping the joints mobile.

4) Pranayama

Prana is energy. By learning the different breathing techniques energy will be shifted, which means blocked energy will be released.

5) Pratyahara

This is the fifth limb of the eight limbs. Pratyahara means 'withdrawal of the senses', going inwards. By going inwards to the self, you will connect to the soul.

6) Dharana

This is the sixth limb and Dharana means 'concentration'. This concentration will lead you into Meditation and to start with would be in the form of concentrating on an object. This object could be within the self, which means for example a Chakra. Or this object could be an external object, like staring at a candle watching the flames and focusing just on the candle. Another example would be to concentrate on a Mantra which is a sacred sound like chanting 'OM'.

7) Dhyana

Dhyana is Meditation and is the seventh limb. This is the stage where the mind stays focused on the chosen object.

8) Samadhi

This is the eighth limb. This is the stage to aspire to and is a state of being totally absorbed with the object. In this state of Meditation you are continually focused and hold this focus for a sustainable time, it is continuous. The mind is peaceful.

By practicing Meditation you will feel a beautiful state of balance and harmony and may experience bliss. You will feel pure divine love in your heart. Self-realizations will come to you and you will connect to the Soul.

Unity of the mind, body and spirit is attainable through this practice.

Chapter 3: Vibhuti Pada - Magical Powers

Chapter 3starts by explaining the last three limbs of Patanjali's eight limbs of Yoga (Astanga Yoga) - Concentration, Meditation and Samadhi (beautiful blissful state) and how the three integrate into Samyana, which is total continuous concentration.

Here we learn of the siddhis, which are the supernatural powers that are a gift to those who connect to The Great Divine. However, there is a warning that this gift could come at a cost - further progress to your spiritual practice. It is easy to become distracted by these powers; this is a lesson in ego. Some people connect deeply to their Spiritual Guides or to Angels, for instance. However, there is a warning to not become too attached to these guides and celestial beings, this is not liberation. You may have beautiful experiences connecting with these allies, but this is not the goal. True transformation takes place when you have a shift in energy, and this cannot be attained through the magic powers.

This shift in energy can be attained through your continued effort to work with your energy, getting to know and understand the esoteric body. Understanding the chakras and connecting deeply with the self will allow healing to take place.

This chapter refers to the fact that once you experience this shift in energy and the magic powers develop, your intuition gets stronger and you may be able to sense not only your own energies, but that of others.

By focusing on our fire energy, our Sun energy within, knowledge of the seven main Chakras will be attained. Not only will you be in touch with these energy centers within, but you may start to sense spiritual energies around you.

Chapter 4: Kaivalya Pada - Liberation

Your spiritual practice is a continuous journey. Kaivalya is freedom - emancipation - liberation; from suffering, from afflictions. You will have learned how to let go of your wounds and past issues.

Chapter 4 is like giving you a 'pat on the back' saying well done for coming this far, but don't give up your practice, your journey has not ended. Incorporate what you have learned into your daily life. You will experience wonderful meditation and possibly out of body experiences but you cannot be in this place 'twenty four seven'. Be in both worlds - have your feet on the ground, and be connected with Spirit.

You have learned to walk in your own power and you understand the concept of mind, body and soul. You know the self, you have done much work and you walk and live in light. Your healing will show in the way you speak, walk and show yourself to the world. Others will feel your beautiful presence and your healing energies will spread to others and out to the Universe.

Once you become a clear channel (through self development

and healing your wounds), you may become a spiritual teacher yourself. Pass what you have learned on to others.

How to achieve Spiritual Power

There are five main ways for you to achieve spiritual power:

Being born with these powers.
Through the use of herbs or drugs.
Chanting mantras.
Devotional practice.
Meditation.

Being born with these powers: we all have the capabilities to tap into the spiritual powers. There are certain people who have these gifts from birth to use to help others. It could be said that these are a gift or the fruits of previous lives. Some may see them as a burden. (To see spirit as a child could be a frightening experience). Others have inherited these gifts from their ancestors.

Through the use of herbs or drugs: many people today think they can fast-track their spiritual experiences by taking drugs to experience hallucination. This is a temporary insight that can be very damaging. (There are natural herbs that can be taken such as Ayahuasca in Peru which can be seen by some as spiritually cleansing).

Chanting mantras: by chanting sacred words and repeating them quietens the mind and can lead to the senses withdrawing, taking you into deep contemplation.

Devotional practice; self-discipline to get you to practice daily. This may be in the form of energy work - exercise, Yoga postures, or Tai Chi. Continued self-study; you have come so far with contemplating the self, now you may be ready to do some soul work; to work at a deeper level with the self.

Meditation; you will have practiced different techniques and now you should know what works for you.

Your practice is becoming more powerful. You find you can meditatemore easily. Your mind is more disciplined. You are connected to nature. You understand the concept of being grounded but also being connected to spirit.

You are in touch with your esoteric body - your own energy system. You can feel grounding energies in your lower chakras. You also feel connected to spirit from your upper chakras. Your energy does not leak out, it flows beautifully like a river.

You learn to channel energy correctly. If someone tries to anger you, you don't hold onto this anger, you let it go. The tyrants around you - those that are judgmental, critical, racist or opinionated don't bother you any more. You have learned to not take on any energy that is harmful to your mind and your spirit.

You are learning to be led by your intuition, the truth, rather than by the ego, the distorted truth, and by this stage you know to follow your heart.

Meditation will diminish the shadow self. Emotions such as lust, greed, fear, jealousy and anger will be subdued.

Your mind learns to let go.

By now you will know your own truths, use your wisdom and learn to live in balance and harmony. You will be free from the dramas of life but at the same time you will be grounded with your energies, as well as connected to Spirit energies.

You will be at peace in the mind and in the heart and will understand the concept of liberation - being free, feeling divine love, joy and happiness.

You can now live with this freedom. You are out of the dark and live in the light. You still have your earthly duties - your family, your work - but you are above all the dramas that exist around you. You have been working at a deep soul level. You have recognized the gifts and freedoms that your family have given you and you have also worked on the limitations and burdens. You see the lessons that life has thrown at you. You have true wisdom and are very knowing. This is freedom.

Now you are walking in your own power. You do not quote from books or from teachers, you speak from your heart. You know your truths and you are now wisdom itself.

You have reached Self-realization.

You are at one with The Great Divine

You are pure consciousness.

Kaivalya - liberation.

Summary

The main points to focus on to help you on your spiritual quest are:

Moving energy in the form of physical movement which can be in the form of Yoga Postures.

Practicingforms of breathing techniques. To focus on the breath, to learn to breathe using the full capacity of the lungs.

Practicing meditation - trying the various types of techniques such as focusing on the breath, using visualizations, working with sound - musical instruments, chanting.

Practicing Svadhyaya - self-study and study of sacred texts. Work on healing your wounds, peel off the layers that have built up over the years developing patterns and holding on to the past, learn to let go. Learn from your challenges and lessons in life.

Be free, at peace, happy and healthy.

Chapter 6

Numerology

Numerology is another way of studying your energies. Numerologists believe that you are born at a certain date and time, not by chance, but to learn important lessons and to do certain work during your lifetime, and that the circumstances and vibrations at the time of your birth will have an influence on your Soul purpose in life and your destiny. Numerology is also a method of character analysis which uses the number of names and birth dates to solve such questions of 'Who am I?' and 'What am I here for?' You will be able to understand yourself more and also those around you.

You can find out your destiny number by doing the following:
Take your date of birth and add each digit up i.e.:

18th January 1962 = 18/1/1962 = 1+ 8+1+1+9+6+2 = 28 = 2+8 = 10
This person is a number 1 with the zero accentuating this one.

2nd October 1995 = 2/10/1995 = 2 + 1 + 0 + 1 + 9 + 9 + 5 = 27= 2+7
= 9
This person is a number 9

Number 1 - Creativity and Confidence
Number one represents masculine energy which means Yang, Man, and ego. In the Tarot major arcana, the number 1 is The Magician. Those with a number one energy tend to be good leaders and good at organizing, and this could be in the home, at

work or a good organizer generally. One is an individual who is capable of great achievement; it is a positive, strong number. If you are working with the positive energies of a one you will tend to be creative, intelligent, courageous, and have good self esteem and confidence. If you are working with the negative energies of a one you could be impatient, impulsive and over confident, which could lead to arrogance and aggression. A negative number one tends to have no energy, rather than the lovely full energy of a positive one. A negative one will often have low Self-esteem and confidence, tending to feeling ill and insecure.

In health matters, ones can be lonely and tend to have illnesses around the head area which means headaches, sinus problems, wisdom teeth problems or depression.

Number 2 - Cooperation and Balance

Number two represents the feminine (she is The High Priestess in the Tarot). If you are a number two, then you are here to learn about cooperation and balance. In the positive aspect of number two you will work in harmony and balance and be very cooperative. You are not a leader like the number one energy, so you are quite happy to follow. You will make an ideal partner and friend and are good at balancing energies, which means you don't take too much energy from others nor do you give too much, you know what balance is and what an equal exchange of energy will mean in a relationship and friendship.

You will be patient and reliable.

If you are working in the negative energies of two then you will be very selfish, shy, ambitionless, fretful and could become a doormat to others.

In health issues, twos tend to have problems with anything that there is two of on the body which means eyes, elbows, arms, knees, etc.

Number 3 - Expression and Sensitivity

Number three represents mother energy (in Tarot the number 3 major arcana card is The Empress). If you are a number three and working with the positive energies, you will probably have a good sense of humor and be sociable. You will be good at expressing yourself and communicating in general and you will be compassionate to yourself as well as others. Threes can be creative and often like working with their hands. As they are good at communicating they often make good teachers, and are good in sales and public relations positions. Singers have often got three in their numbers.

A number three working with the negative energies will be fickle, flirtatious, critical of others and themselves, overly sensitive, non-communicative or bad at expressing themselves.

If a three is in the first number, which means the third of the month, then it *could* mean mother issues. These issues could be in the form of control, not getting on with mother, mother not there for support, or the opposite, a mummy's child - spoiled.

With health issues, threes tend to have problems around the throat which could mean sore throat, thyroid, clenched jaw, neck and shoulder tensions.

Number 4 - Stability and Wisdom

Number four represents father energy (in Tarot the number 4 major arcana card is The Emperor). A positive four is often a 'salt of the earth' type. They literally like being earthed by gardening and pottering around tending to beautiful flowers. They love color and are often artists. They make good friends and can take the good with the bad in a person and accept it. They are loyal and are normally quite grounded types which means they are not wanderers, they like strong foundations in the form of their home, relationship, career and life generally. They are logical, focused and know what they want from life. They know their own minds and are often wise. They are often quite laid back types.

A number four working in the negative can be ungrounded, impatient, inflexible; they are opinionated and won't listen to others' point of view and can often be domineering. They are insecure and often get despondent. They could also be too loyal for their own good or a bit too stuck in a rut with their ways and not open to change. They don't deal with stress very well and will often suffer from health issues around the heart area.

If a four is in the first number of the date of birth, which means the fourth of the month, then this *could* relate to father issues. This could mean father not there for support, a dominating father, not getting on with father or the opposite, a daddy's child - spoiled.

With health matters, fours often have issues around the heart area, and when they are working negatively and not dealing with stress they can get blood pressure issues.

Number 5 - Freedom and Discipline

Number five represents freedom and discipline which means they are often free spirits, loving freedom in aspects of their lives and having problems with discipline and being given rules and regulations and told what to do.

A positive number five will be independent, fun loving, energetic, humorous, adaptable to change. They often make good writers as they have an active imagination as well as being front people in business as they are good with words, being quick thinking. Fives are free spirits and love adventure. They do need constant stimulation so a good match will have to be found in a relationship in order for attention to be kept alive. They can be likened to the butterfly; they like to flit around.

In Tarot, the number five of the major arcana is The Hierophant which is the master healer and teacher. Once a five has sorted out their own life, their wounds, and are in touch with the Soul, they make really good teachers and healers. Often they are working from their own experiences.

In the negative, a five will have so much going on in their lives that they scatter their energy all over the place which means their health could suffer due to lost energy. Because they need stimulation, they have a low boredom threshold so can be quite needy in a relationship. They need to learn to be comfortable with themselves and their own company or they can become totally dependent on others. Because their minds are so active they tend to be worriers and don't always cope very well with stress and can often turn to other forms of help such as drugs or alcohol.

In health matters they can scatter their energy all over the place which means they become tired and generally run down. They are prone to asthma and really need to calm their active minds with meditation.

Number 6 - Harmony and balance

After the lively number five, the number six represents peace and harmony. They are often the peacemakers in the household, the ones who hold the peace and stop arguments from getting out of hand. At work they are diplomatic and can offer much needed balance.

A positive number six will be unselfish, giving strength and comfort in their relationships, which tend to be long lasting. Home is very important to them and is their immediate concern. They make great parents. They are caring and nurturing and emotionally strong; they learn to live in balance and harmony. They have natural healing abilities and love helping others. They are good with their hands and often like jobs where they can be creative.

In the Tarot the number six is The Lovers which means the card of relationships, the balance of male and female energies.

The negative number six will be selfish and critical - of the Self and others. They can have blinkered vision, particularly with home and family, they can be possessive in a relationship and with their children, they find it hard to let go of their responsibilities and allow a child grow up and do their own thing.

If the birth numbers contain a six and a seven, for example 7th June (sixth month) 1955 then it could mean being at 'sixes and sevens' with the Self, with inner conflict and being out of harmony and balance.

In health matters, sixes can often have back issues and problems around the lower abdomen, which may mean the reproductive area. This would only be the case if their energies are out of balance and harmony.

Number 7 - Focus

The number seven represents success and development (in the Tarot the seven card is The Chariot). The challenge for the number seven is knowing when success has been found and to not continue seeking for more.

A positive number seven will be focused in all aspects of their lives, their relationship, their career and where they are heading in general. Once this focus is maintained then success often follows. They are often psychic which means they read for others to give them guidance and help. They have the natural ability of a clairvoyant, one who sees, and clairaudience, one who hears. They often want to help others in a healing way but will neglect their own needs. They need to learn to trust in themselves. They make good teachers and if a number five appears in their numbers then this teaching could be on a spiritual level. Sevens appreciate nature and love being outdoors, they love traveling.

A seven in the negative will be unfocused and their lives will be hectic and messy. They can become loners and become too introspective making them moody and depressed. They are not great at getting balance in their lives but that is their challenge. Others find them unapproachable at times and don't know how to take them.

In health matters they are prone to joint problems and

anything to do with bones.

Number 8 - Abundance and Power

Number eights are here to learn to use their power in a positive way. In the Tarot the number eight card is Strength which represents using diplomacy and tact to get what you want in life rather than brute force and ignorance.

A positive eight will be balanced between the spirit energies and the material earth energies. They will also be balanced with their own energies and in particular their emotions. They will be strong, powerful and assertive but at the same time they understand human nature and are known humanitarians. They are there to lend a hand and will often give to charity with the right intent. They are courageous and brave. They are often successful people in terms of business and money and are in control of their lives.

A negative number eight may have extreme swings of wealth and famine. They could have control issues, either being too controlling or being controlled by others, and that is their challenge. They are often either too materialistic and not in touch with their spiritual self or to the other extreme, obsessed with spirituality and not getting on in the material world. If they are out of balance and harmony, they tend to do things tothe extreme. Stress can be an issue when they are out of balance.

With health matters, eights tend to have stress related issues such as asthma, high blood pressure, lung issues and circulation issues.

Number 9 - Integrity and Wisdom

If you are a number nine you may be a leader with great spiritual aspirations. A positive number nine has great wisdom and, once in touch with their own Soul, will often go on to help others. They have leadership qualities and possess a variety of talents. It is said that nines will rise like a phoenix out of the ashes, once they have healed their own wounds. They can be very spiritual and love helping others. They are often intelligent, courageous, loving, passionate, and love seeking. They are often called old souls, which means they have had many lives and carry a lot of karma which is not necessarily bad but depends on actions from past lives. A positive nine can become extremely powerful and have great integrity, being whole, pure and honest.

So if you have a nine in your numbers, as everyone from the last century does from the year number which starts with 19, then karma will be an issue.

A negative nine will not cope with the challenges that this number brings and they can be very fragile. Nines can turn to other forms of support such as drugs and alcohol and can go to the heights and depths in life. They can become negative and depressive, which is why they fall back on the drugs and drink.

In Tarot the number nine is The Hermit, which means scope for spiritual growth and possibly a leader in this field. The Hermit reminds us that at times we need to be alone in order to evolve.

In health matters, nines tend to be like an old creaking chair which means not one ailment but many.

0 - Inner Gifts

People with a zero in their numbers i.e.: 19/10s, 28/10s, 37/10s, 46/10s 20/2s, 30/3s and 40/4s have the gifts, or potential to manifest these qualities in greater abundance. The zero intensifies the other number. So if someone's destiny number comes down to a ten then the zero will intensify the qualities of the number one.

Master numbers in numerology

In numerology there are three main master numbers, 11, 22 and 33, which means that their destiny numbers will be one of these three. You do not break these down, which means 11 does not become 2, 22 does not become 4, and 33 does not become 6. These people have all the qualities of the master number, which means 11 has the qualities of the one number, 22 has the qualities of the two number and 33 has the qualities of three, plus the following qualities:

Master Number 11

A greater degree of awareness is possible. Elevens have lots of creative energy which needs to be channeled correctly. Elevens are often here to deal with prejudice.

They may choose careers such as teachers, social workers - anything that deals with the community or working with large groups of people. Elevens are big carers of the community. Elevens have the ability of mass communication, group effort, intuition, cooperation, impersonality. They are very creative people.

The possible negative aspect would be the same as for the one, but also the eleven should stay as 11 but if the person is not rising to the challenge of this master number, then it could mean they are then in the two energy: 11 = 1+1 = 2.

Master Number 22

Their path is focused on development and expression on national or planetary levels - they are often involved in areas of life that affect the entire nation in which they live - Presidents, Premiers, Kings & Queens, Politicians. They make decisions that affect large numbers of people. They could be involved in the military.

They are often extremely talented and powerful people with a big influence over others.

Key words are expansive power, universal vision, structural awareness, big!

They could become manipulative and domineering.

They are working on a high vibration - often difficult to keep grounded - here to teach on a transcending level.

Master Number 33

For example, overall numbers are 33/6. They are often intuitive, creative and wise - teaching with wisdom and deep knowledge. They need to keep grounded. They are working with issues of perfectionism, emotional expression and self-doubt. Often 33s are very in touch with their feminine energies and perhaps their lesson is to balance this out with their male side.

Splitting the numbers down into Stages of Growth

Stages of growth and vibrations can be split into three stages: first stage - childhood - the day of the month; second stage - early adulthood - the month number; and the third stage - later adulthood - the year. These numbers can be broken down to a single digit to get more detail.

18 / 1 / 1962

18 = day of month - 1 + 8 = 9 = childhood years

1 = month = adulthood years

1962 = year = 1 + 9 + 6 + 2 = 18 = 1 + 8 = 9 later adulthood (45+)

Numerological Years

You can also find out what year you are in, in terms of numerology.

To work out your current year

To work out what year is the current vibration, take the day of the month from your birth date, plus the month number and plus the current year i.e.:

18/1/1962 = 1+ 8 + 1 + current year i.e.: 2009 = 2 + 0 + 0 + 9 = year = 21 = 3

This person, from the date of their birthday, is in a 3 year in 2009.

Number 1 Year

Number one year brings new beginnings or new opportunities. You will probably want to make moves - this is a very exciting year. If you are impulsive - think it through! This is a good year to start all things new. Number one is the number of leadership - take the reins. It is a good year for promotion. Put all plans into action - especially business ideas. Travel is likely this year - it will bring you new experiences. New people will come onto the scene - cultivate each friendship - they may be lifelong. Keep an open mind - get out of any ruts - set the pace for the 9 year cycle. Be positive.

Number 2 Year

Number two year is for decisions, choices, crossroads. After a year of new ventures, number two is a year to sit back and relax and wait for some of the results of last year's efforts. You will definitely see some rewards. Look into any offers; there may be a few surprises. A year to cooperate. A good year for new friends - if unmarried it could include your mate-to-be. Beware of an unsavory sort. If you experience any difficulties at home or in business, use patience and courage.

Number 3 Year

Number three year is good on a career level. It is a year for carrying out intentions and ambitions. A very creative year. A year for fun, socializing and pleasure. Look out for good contacts. Three is a symbol for self-expression. It is a good time to 'pop the question' if contemplating marriage. A good time to sell. Watch how you say things when expressing yourself. Writing is a good outlet. Spend time and money on yourself - new clothes, new hairstyle. The three vibration brings romance and affection. Three is the number of sex - sensuality will be increased which could lead to passionate relationships or an affair - sexual awakening.

Number 4 Year

Number four year is a year for laying new foundations for the future. You may feel insecure, may be working under pressure OR placing Yourself under pressure. This is the time to get busy and knuckle down to work. It is not known as a great year for financial reward - but you will reap the rewards eventually. One-to-three years are preliminary cycles and now you must really get down to work. You should have goals and work towards them. Big returns will come to you later. The four vibration is one of strength and building. Foundations will be laid for the future. This applies to relationships as well as financial and material matters.

Number 5 Year

Work pressure does not let up. It is a year for reorganization. You may not like this as it could make you feel restless. This cycle finally breaks the pattern of hard work. Five is symbol of change and progress. Travel is well favored - maybe a well earned holiday. It is a good year for communication. Something unexpected may occur - take the challenge. There is a warning to watch your finances. Romance may enter your life, but there could be a patchy beginning. Not a good year to make any permanent associations, business or otherwise. Don't sign anything binding. This is a year to watch health, try not to scatter energy, stay focused. Good times are coming; meanwhile enjoy the social and exciting 5 year.

Number 6 Year

This is a year for commitments, conceptions and families. On the negative side, relationships can split if that is what is meant to be. Affairs of the home will be uppermost in your mind. If married, you will be content in that relationship, if single you will dwell on thoughts of home, a mate, children. Six is the number of domesticity - harmonize surroundings of work and home - make this personalized. You will feel a need for permanence which will make you want to buy a home or re-decorate / refurbish. Arts and culture include the vibration of number six. Paint, sing, learn an instrument. You will be a comfort to those around you. The six vibration is one of protection; you will not be plagued with business or financial problems. Make your usual effort and all will be well and comfortable.

Number 7 Year

Number seven year is building for the eight year, sowing the seeds. In this year, if you stay focused, you will nurture the seeds for the future. This could be a year for travel (remember the Tarot Chariot card). Great understanding and peace should be yours, as it is a year of deep contemplation and mental pursuits. Moments of solitude will be welcomed, but do not be over analytical. It is quite a slow year in both business and personal life. Studies in mysticism, psychic phenomena, religion, etc. will interest you (related to the magical number seven and the seven chakras). Your social life could be slow; you may prefer to be by yourself. Distance plays a part - if you have a long distance friend or relative, keep in touch. A good year for creation. Be prepared for surprise gifts; inheritances are apt to show in this year.

Number 8 Year

If you have sown your seeds, now you can see them grow and you will reap the rewards that patience and nurturing can bring. This can be a year of pressure, but it can be a good year finan-cially, but only if you have put your energy in earlier. It is a year to conserve energies healthwise. If you had goals and ambitions, this is the year where you should see the benefits. Eight symbolizes fulfillment of material goals you seek. Business is controlled by the number eight and you should prosper especially well in this year. Take the lead in your business affairs but share the rewards. Important decisions will be made, important people will be met. As a woman it is a good year for going after your man.

Number 9 Year

This is a year of endings; this is the end of a cycle, ready for the following number one year. It is a year of sorting out. Clear the attic AND the mind. Have direction; this is a powerful year for changing jobs. Now is the time to put an end to all lingering relationship, affairs or businesses that have not proved profitable. Number nine requires that you put the past behind you and prepare for a whole new beginning ready for the number one year. Put all your affairs in order. In business, it is time to secure or eliminate. You may be bored with hobbies or people; time to 'clean up'. Get any nagging health issues cleared up so you do not take them into your new cycle. You should be fresh and ready for your new challenges and cycle. Determine where to concentrate your efforts this year. A year to follow your destiny.

Chapter 7

Tarot - The Journey of Life
Seventy Eight Steps to Enlightenment

The History of Tarot

Tarot cards are a powerful tool of self-empowerment and a good reading can be enormously beneficial. But Tarot is often surrounded by fear and mystery which probably goes way back in history to when the Church had great power over people. It takes years to learn the cards and the meanings behind the symbolism. Tarot connects you with your journey through life, which means birth, growth, relationships, inner wisdom, ego, light and dark, wholeness and death. A reading will often show you things you already know but will bring the thoughts into perspective and will offer you guidance and clarity. This is a really useful tool when used correctly.

You can do readings for yourself but if you are at a major crossroads in life and are confused and unsure as to which direction you are heading, a professional reading can be really helpful and at times life changing.

There is a lot of speculation and mystery surrounding the facts of where the Tarot actually came from and when it first started, but it originally goes back to ancient times. It is believed that the ancient Egyptians used symbolism to express their spiritual beliefs and their every day life. It is also thought that gypsies introduced the Tarot when they reached Europe in the fifteenth century. The earliest preserved set of Tarot cards is the Visconti-Sforza deck produced in the mid fifteenth century. As early as the eighth century, a form of the Tarot was thought to have been used by the Saracens.

A rather interesting theory is that the Tarot contained the

coded symbols that could communicate the Templars' secret teachings to their novices without raising suspicion from the Catholic Church. Unfortunately, during the persecution of the Templars the true purpose of the cards was apparently revealed and the Tarot was declared a heretical device and outlawed. In the 20th century, the Tarot was used in a number of esoteric, theosophical and secret societies.

The Tarot has seen many changes throughout its history but overall its essence remains the same, as it has true wisdom of truth. It provides the link between our logical mind and our true Self and shows a connection between mankind and the Great Divine.

There are hundreds of types of Tarot decks. One of the most popular decks is the Rider-Waite and this is a good deck to start with (Rider-Waite Universal is widely used). The Aquarian and Morgan-Greer decks are offshoots of the Rider-Waite and are again good decks to start with.

When you choose a deck, you will be drawn to a particular one. Use your intuition. Hold the deck. Look through it and look at the back. Does everything appeal to you? What energy does the deck give to you? How does it feel size-wise? Take all these things into consideration before you select your deck.

There are 78 cards in a deck, consisting of: 22 Major Arcana and 56 Minor Arcana. There are four suits, which also relate to the elements - Pentacles (Earth), Swords (Air), Cups (Water) and Wands (Fire). In each suit there is an ace, the numbers 2-10, Page, Knight, Queen and King.

(Arcane = mysterious, secret, understood by few).

Remember, the knowledge is within. A good Tarot Reader will never tell you how to run your life or make decisions for you; it is up to you to use your free-will in life.

The 22 Cards of the Major Arcana - 22 steps to The Great Divine

0 - The Fool

A young man is standing on the edge of a cliff looking up to the bright, sunny sky. He wears boots and a brightly decorated tunic. In one hand he holds a white rose representing innocence, and in the other a Dick Whittington-style bag, tied to a stick which is resting on his shoulder. Beside him is an excitable white dog, representing how dogs are instinctive animals, and the message could be about following your instincts on a situation going on around you.

The Fool brings the excitement of something new. You are about to embark on a journey and this new energy could be in the form of a new relationship, a new job, there may be new energies around, or you may be going on a trip. The Fool is naïve; there is lots to learn but the new journey needs to be made so that growth can be experienced. The Fool is full of energy and enthusiasm, which represents the energy and excitement felt when embarking on something new. The cliff represents the danger of the unknown, the jump into the darkness, and the Fool seems oblivious to the potential dangers that could await, but that is not always a bad thing as if we knew the consequences of all our actions then we wouldn't take these leaps in life. The Fool is looking for new challenges or adventures. The white rose is the symbol representing rebirth and innocence. This is time to trust yourself and your natural instincts, and at times take a leap of faith in life.

1 - The Magician

A man dressed in a white tunic and a red robe stands holding one hand pointing towards the earth and one hand pointing up towards the sky. Behind him is a yellow background and in front of him is a table with the four suits represented; a Cup, a

Pentacle, a Sword and a Wand.

The key word is transformation, of ideas into action. The Magician represents male energy - action energies - ego, strong energy. When the Magician appears, it is time to focus on goals. It is also time to use the intellect. Perhaps a decision needs to be made concerning which direction to take, and this is represented by the four tools, the Sword, Wand, Pentacle and Cup. The wand directed towards the sky represents connection to the Divine, while the Magician's left hand is directed to the ground, to earth. This reminds us to have a balance of both these energies in life. The lemniscate (figure of eight) above his head also points out a need to connect the physical (or seen) with the spiritual (or unseen) realms and to recognize how divine force expresses itself through our personal actions. Higher wisdom is brought down to a practical level. On the table are the four symbols of the four suits; this represents the different directions life has to offer. Selecting the Cup would suggest that love and relationships are paramount in that person's life, while the Pentacles might indicate a desire for wealth to dominate. The Wand might suggest a wish to create, while the Sword could point to a desire to fight.

Yellow is the color of the intellect and this logical part of our brain gives clarity of thought. Yellow is also the color of the sun, of warmth and giving, confidence and happiness - very uplifting. Red can be seen as representing passions, could be aggression. White can be seen as representing purity.

This card could represent self-employment or a student who is graduating.

The Magician is your inner guide.

2 - The High Priestess

A serene looking woman sits on a throne dressed in a white tunic with a blue cloak. On the front of her tunic is a white cross and at her feet is a crescent moon. On her head she wears a hat representing the three phases of the moon; waxing, full and waning. She sits between two pillars, one black and one white. She holds a scroll with the word 'Tora' on it.

The High Priestess represents The Divine Feminine. She shows the balance of dark and light in this world, as well as the harmony between the spiritual and the mundane. She has deep feelings of personal and universal love. The scroll contains the laws of the universe, the core truths that lie at the heart of all spiritual and moral teachings. TORA (Torah), which is written on the scroll, is the Jewish book of law - wisdom, knowledge, eternal law and mystery. She is the memory, the storehouse of all your successes, failures, dreams and fantasies. She gets inspiration through meditation. She is in tune with the Moon - feminine energies, intuition, cycles (women's cycles are the same as the Moon cycle - 28 days).

The white pillar with the letter J for Jakin represents masculine energy (sun, ego, logical mind, practical matters and courage). The black pillar with the letter B for Boaz represents the feminine principle (imagination, intuition, compassion and nurturing). The pillars represent duality and opposites. The feminine principle cannot exist without its counterpart, the masculine principle. The pillars remind us of the duality of our gender (the mixed energies of male and female within ourselves) and the duality of life - Yin and Yang and how we need both of these energies to exist.

The cross represents her spiritual side - healing energies and nurturing. She could be pointing out psychic skills that you may have, or do you have caring, nurturing skills such as a nurse or in the caring industry? Blue is often represented as a healing color.

The High Priestess asks you to look into your unconscious, trust your intuition or your gut feeling, and to be open to dreams and imagination.

3 The Empress

The Empress is the second feminine principle of the Tarot and represents the Mother energy. A young woman sits on a throne surrounded by nature - beautiful trees, an abundance of the beautiful things that Mother Earth provides us - portraying prospering, plenty and well-being. The Empress represents birth and the full flow of fertility and pregnancy; this could be literally or symbolically. She holds a scepter which is a symbol of the divine and of royalty - the Queen of Nature. The tiara consists of 12 stars representing the 12 astrological signs. The four elements of the signs are part of Mother Nature, and this reminds us of the need to be in balance, to complement these energies, to preserve harmony and peace in the natural world. Her necklace has seven pearls, which links to the seven chakras. When the chakras are all in harmony with each other, the body is well balanced and healthy which is how The Empress is portrayed. The reverse would be appropriate if the chakras were out of balance. The shield has the sign of Venus, the ruler of the signs Libra and Taurus. Venus is associated with love, the arts and beauty.

The Empress can mean that plans are turning into reality. Goals are being achieved - projects that have been started (given birth to) are starting to grow. The Empress represents domestic harmony and stability and also creativity.

4 The Emperor

A mature man is seen sitting on a large, solid throne adorned in red robes, with armor over his legs and feet. His feet are firmly on the ground. Behind him is a bright orange background representing fire energy. He wears a crown and a long, gray beard, representing wisdom.

The Emperor is an image of Father energy and male authority - the masculine. Whereas our intuitive sides are feminine energy, the masculine side is the ego. The Emperor is seated on a throne symbolizing power, possibly wealth, leadership, wisdom and confidence. He inspires you to lead those who look to you for guidance - he has wisdom through experience, is organized, has knowledge and is responsible. On the negative side he could be seen as dominant and controlling, stubborn, or maybe he shies away from responsibility.

The Emperor shows success through self-discipline and practical efforts. He shows a time of great stability and order in your life. Depending on other cards in the layout he could mean that responsible people such as policemen, judges and bosses, etc. may play a role in your life. It could mean the relationship with your Father may have issues which are either positive or negative.

The Emperor reminds you to adopt a pragmatic approach to life in order to succeed, and of the need for self-discipline to achieve goals.

5 The Hierophant

A priest is sitting on a throne between two pillars adorned in a bright red robe with three crosses. He has two disciples looking up to him. He holds a three-pronged staff representing mind, body and spirit.

The Hierophant is known as the master healer and teacher - both to the Self and then to others. The Hierophant teaches ideas and traditions that have proven their worth. The keys unlock doors for exploration and teaching. When The Hierophant appears, perhaps it is time to develop a philosophy to live by, to set standards of how you wish to lead your life and to follow your beliefs, and also to respect people of all backgrounds and cultures. The Hierophant is a wise and successful elder who is a preserver and carrier of spiritual tradition.

He is a Spiritual Mentor, representing the search that propels many of us to find spiritual or religious meaning in our lives in whichever direction we may choose to go. The Hierophant becomes the teacher, the guide or mentor who uses the mind to uncover mysteries. He learns through seeking, reading and looks to the spoken word for answers.

Spiritual direction and guidance is the Hierophant's mission. He also reminds us to make up our own minds and not follow blindly any kind of doctrine or preaching without questioning and experiencing for ourselves.

The Hierophant can appear in readings at times of marriage - showing the bride and groom conforming to the society rules of family values. It could also mean a struggle within a group and the need to break free as you may feel imprisoned by rules, regulations conventions and traditions.

6 The Lovers

This is a card of relationships, both with the Self and others. The scenery reminds us of the biblical representation of Adam and Eve, with a naked man and woman looking up to an Angel. Behind the man is the Tree of Life or Tree of Consciousness, which represents the masculine principle and the material world. Behind the woman is the Tree of Knowledge, representing the feminine principle and the spiritual world. The snake represents our liberator because it forces us to weigh the possibilities presented to us, for us to make a choice. These choices should be thought through and the consequences weighed up. The Angel represents healing and support. The Lovers could represent the situation of a relationship. Six is a number of relationships, harmony and balance.

The Lovers is a card of choice; there may be a decision to make involving feelings and emotions. It reminds us to use our intuition, be in touch with, and listen to, the true Self rather than the ego or intellect.

The card could represent a relationship and issues that need to be looked at.

7 The Chariot

A young man rides in a chariot led by two sphinxes, one white and one black. He is dressed in some armor and a tunic showing the signs of the zodiac. The chariot is covered in a blue fabric with stars on it, showing that perhaps it is time to study the mystics (perhaps the spiritual self, the chakras, etc.) or could represent someone who is psychic.

The Chariot is a card of movement and development, of victory and triumph. It is a time to move from the past into the future. The card shows he has the ability to use consciousness and purposeful concentration to control the sphinxes, to use focus. He has the potential for leadership, responsibility and authority. Success is achieved through initiative and effort. Perhaps a clear sense of purpose is needed, to resist temptation in order to move forward.

When the Chariot appears, this is not a time to relax and step back, it is a time of action. It can also represent movement in the form of moving home or locations.

This card could also represent someone who lacks focus, who lets the sphinxes go in different directions, rather than working together.

8 Strength

A calm looking woman is seen taming a wild lion. She is dressed in a white dress decorated with a garland of flowers around her waist and head. There is a lemniscate (figure of eight) above her head and the background is a pale yellow representing the mind - using intelligence in a situation, and in this case taming the lion with gentle persuasion but assertiveness, so fear is not shown.

The Strength card reminds us to learn to tame the beast within. The lion represents our animal instincts and desires. The lemniscate indicates a transformative moment coming into a time of inner balance and strength. The lion seems tame - and this is through gentleness and compassion, rather than control and manipulation. This woman has good health and strength and has achieved this through spiritual practices which have given her harmony and balance. Spiritual strength can lead to healing in both body and mind.

9 The Hermit

A mature man is seen standing on top of a snowy mountain dressed in gray robes, holding a wooden wand in one hand and holding up a lantern with a brightly lit star, which represents the Soul. The background is pale blue, a color of healing.

The Hermit heralds a time for reflection and introspection in the quest for deeper understanding. His solitude can be a strength and his patience brings peace and acceptance. He brings higher knowledge from the past, which can shed new light on your present situation. The Hermit can be thought of as a teacher, counselor, therapist or Spirit Guide, whichever role appeals to you when you seek advice. The answers, though, must come from within. When the Hermit appears in a reading, it could be time to take some time out, maybe a holiday, or to break free for a little while from your daily routine. Self-development is emphasized here - perhaps a time to meditate, maybe. The Hermit is a card of maturity, learning and growth. It could also represent time for a self-development healing course and self-enlightenment.

10 The Wheel of Fortune

A wheel is resting on the back of the God Anubis, with a snake representing transformation, to the left. In each corner are creatures representing the four elements and they are studying a book.

Everything in life goes through change cycles, and when the Wheel of Fortune appears in a reading it is likely that change and possibly confrontation is imminent. It could represent a struggle, but with some recognition of the problem a solution will be found. The Wheel gives us a chance to look back on things - the last cycle, look at patterns, what have we learned and how can we move forward - what changes do we need to instigate? The Wheel can represent good luck and fortune and new opportunity.

The Wheel is the cycle of life, constantly in motion, changing events. We all experience the motion of the Wheel and its good and bad influences. The four gold-winged creatures represent the four elements – eagle, water; lion, fire; bull, earth; angel, air. The creature with the head of a jackal is the god Anubis, guiding the dead souls and bringing new life. As from death comes rebirth, from change and death of old patterns new patterns arise and new opportunities have to be taken.

11 Justice

An authoritative-looking person is sitting on a throne representing power between two pillars representing balance. This person is holding a set of scales in the left hand and an upright sword in his right hand. He is dressed in a rich red and green robe and is wearing a crown. Behind him is a veil of purple representing divine wisdom.

Justice is the principle of fairness. The Justice card shows it is a time for evaluation - weighing of any situation where the pros and cons should be considered before making a decision. The sword represents air - mental energy - so much thought should be put in. The red cloak represents the color of action - our actions are the consequence of our thinking. The green cape represents the fertility of thoughts. Without thoughts, actions won't take place. The emphasis here is to think of the consequences of any actions. Our decisions and actions will shape our future. Absolute honesty must be used for the right decision to be made.

Justice can also indicate a legal situation or legal documents such as marriage, divorce, job contracts, loans, enrolment into education, etc.

12 The Hanged Man

A young person is seen hanging upside down, being tethered to a tree by his foot. He wears red tights, which could suggest grounding, and a blue tunic. He has a bright halo around his head, representing realizations and enlightenment.

The Hanged Man suggests that we look at a situation from a different perspective - in a different way. Look at all options and angles, and before making your decision give it much thought. Also, see things from other people's point of view. If you are in conflict with someone, then this card suggests not being too obstinate with your views, but being broad minded and open to how others see things. This is not a time to make a rash decision - give it time. Perhaps look at yourself from a different angle. Maybe it is time to look inside the Self, to do some Soul searching and some self-study. It also could be someone in limbo. Perhaps it is a time of nothing happening, which can be frustrating. It often represents some peace in life is on its way after a difficult struggle - be still and reflect on your past actions.

13 Death

A skeleton is seen adorned in a full suit of armor, riding a beautiful white horse. He is carrying a flag decorated with a white rose on a black background. A priest is seen pleading with the rider, and a young woman can't bear to face him, almost as if she is afraid to face the situation. An elderly man is lying on the floor and a child looks up to the horse and rider, looking as if he is the only one dealing with the situation. In the background the sun is rising between two pillars.

The Death card represents a time of change, of new opportunities and transformation. The wooden scythe represents ending cycles. Natural changes in life can bring about transformation and renewal and the figures in the card show that some are better at dealing with these changes than others. Something in a person's life is changing; depending on circumstances, it could be sad or a welcome relief i.e.: end of a relationship, end of school, end of a job, end of single life to marriage (or vice versa). The ending needs to be acknowledged, accepted and mourned, and then it is time to move on. In films or novels, this card is often portrayed as someone dying. Depending on the other cards in the layout, it might be the case that loss has been experienced.

14 Temperance

An Angel is seen standing with one foot in the water, representing the intuitive side of us, and one foot on the ground, representing being grounded with our energies and how we need a balance in life of the spiritual and the material. The Angel carries two golden cups and is pouring water from one to the other. In the background is a golden crown representing wisdom and enlightenment.

The key word for Temperance is moderation. Nothing should exist in extreme i.e.: if the soil around a plant is too dry, it should be moistened, too wet, it should be dried. Nothing should be too hot or too cold. This could be a time to bring moderation into life generally; perhaps this is a reminder that you could be overdoing things and need time for re-balancing energies, which could mean getting away for a period of time. The time is ripe for discussion, for sharing feelings. Temperance reminds us not to discard the past, preserve the best aspects of it, and find new and creative uses for them in the present. Pouring water without spilling it demonstrates self-control. Similar to The Hierophant, this card is about meditation and balancing on a higher spiritual level. A time to look at whether you are possibly being self-centered, out of harmony, having mood swings, showing impatience or a lack of self-control. A time for moderation, compromise, and harmonious partnership.

15 The Devil

A half-man and half-beast is seen over-shadowing a man and a woman who are chained, albeit loosely chained. The background is very dark and the creature is carrying a burning staff in his left hand and he holds up his right hand, which bears a cross.

The Devil looks scary, but is there to help you recognize your shadow side and its heavy burden on you. There is something blocking your energy, but these blocks can be looked at and worked on and then removed, so you can continue to grow. These shadow aspects (also seen by some as dark energies) can be anything negative from addictions to drugs, alcohol or sex. It could also mean being stuck in patterns from the past and there being an opportunity to look at these patterns, to heal old wounds in order for you to feel free and liberated. The Devil can represent over-materialization - someone who is stuck solely in a materialistic life - the only important things to them are material possessions - big house, flash car, etc. In other words, there is nothing wrong with rewarding yourself for your hard work with material possessions, as long as you realize that owning these things solely will not bring you happiness, and there is more to life.

The symbol above the head represents the negative noise in our heads that distracts us from creative endeavors. This negative voice can sabotage you and is destructive to your own power. This card could also represent someone in your life who is trying to take your power, trying to control you, possibly. So the main theme with the Devil is negative blocks that hinder growth, but they can be removed and the energy released.

16 The Tower

The Tower card shows a tower structure on top of a mountain with fire coming out of the windows and from the top. Lightning is striking and two people are seen falling off. The sky is a moody, midnight blue and there are golden drops, possibly representing tears.

The Tower speaks for itself - the top exploding with fire and lightning, people falling off and a feeling that your head is going to explode with all the worry and grief. The top of the Tower could be seen as the crown chakra and how we overload our mind with negative thoughts. It is time to have a 'spring clean' and this could be mentally, emotionally, physically, or actually cleaning the old clutter away in the home. It is time for old ways to be let go of and to make way for new. Existing modes of thinking must be shattered.

If the Tower appears it means that while you could be going through a bad time, or have recently experienced a difficult time, then the good news is that new energy is on the way and it is time for a change in direction.

17 The Star

A lovely peaceful card following the energetic Tower. The Star shows a naked lady pouring water from each hand. Above her is a golden star with seven white stars.

A lovely positive card and considered to be the 'wish card'. After The Tower, The Star gives us hope for the future. It has a lovely optimistic feeling, giving us strength to carry on even if life is difficult. It is a card of balance, time to rebalance energies. She is stabilization and peace. She inspires us to develop inner peace and calm - perhaps through meditation, linking with spiritual energies. It also could be someone who is suffering from loss of self-esteem, loss of hope on a more negative note.

The yellow star represents hope and guidance from God, Buddha, Spirit Guides or whatever your beliefs are. The smaller stars could represent the seven main chakras. The bird - an Ibis was the symbol of Thoth - the ancient Egyptian God of Time and keeper of the Akashic records and the patron of healers. The Akashic records are believed to contain a record of the complete life of every being on earth that lives or has ever lived since the beginning of time. So generally this is a card of happiness, spiritual love, peace, protection, renewed health, growth and optimism.

18 The Moon

This card shows the sun and moon energies together. There is a sun eclipsed by the moon with golden drops possibly representing tears. There are two pillars for balance and two hounds looking up to the sky which is a moody, dark blue.

The Moon reflects a time of confusion which should be allowed rather than avoided. The confusion should be given time to sort itself out. Creativity should evolve and not be forced. Mood swings should be allowed and will pass. The Moon represents our inner feminine energy; this card stirs up deep feelings and emotions. Perhaps it is a time to confront our inner self - our emotions, maybe our shadow side, our dark energies such as fear, anger, etc.

When the Moon appears in a reading it is a time of intuition and for psychic awareness to be awakened. It could be a time of confusion, but patience and reflection will result in clarity. It could also mean though that someone is too introspective, which will result in mood swings and depression. The dogs could represent fears, and maybe it is time to confront these fears. The crayfish is trying to deliver us a message by coming out of the water. The path emerging from the pool represents the way to take - the spiritual path - to reach Self-realization.

19 The Sun

A young child is seen astride a beautiful white horse. He carries an orange flag and behind him is a gray brick wall. The sun is shining brightly and sunflowers are in full bloom.

With the Moon representing our feminine side of intuition, emotions, nurturing, cycles, dark and reflection, the Sun represents our masculine side of ego, confidence, fire and action, and light.

The Sun serves as an energy source for all earthly creatures, sending out rays of creativity and spiritual renewal for you to use. It suggests a time of optimism, celebration, cheerfulness and enthusiasm - the rays bring elation. The sun provides you with the vital energy you need to achieve your goals. The sun depicts the merging of the two energies of male and female so that rebirth will take place.

It could be a time to listen to your inner child - perhaps a time of being afraid, failing to acknowledge or listen to your inner child, not trusting anyone, feeling burned out or as if we are merely surviving rather than thriving. The gray wall represents the limit within which one must keep, otherwise the Sun may prove destructive - too much fire energy will burn, parching crops, drying rivers, killing our source of life.

Celebrate and share your emotional abundance with others. Face the ways you promote closeness, or avoid it, in your relationships.

Generally a card of optimism, vitality, confidence, joy, prosperity, masculine energy. Also of good health, achievement, marriage, friendship, appreciation of life and creativity.

20 Judgment

A naked family is seen reaching up to The Divine; they are standing in coffin-like structures upon water. Above them is an Angel getting their attention by blowing a trumpet.

Judgment tells us clearly that a cycle is ending and that preparation for a new stage of growth must be undertaken. Rebirth and liberation is emphasized and the time has come to reap the rewards of past actions. The card announces a milestone in your development. It is likely that major changes and improvements will take place. It is a time to understand your journey in life up until now and to learn from experiences, challenges and trials presented to you. A call from within reaches you and you are pushed to make some important changes in your life. You must see reality with wide open eyes instead of tinted glasses. New opportunities and beginnings are likely to be presented to you. Old situations and behaviors have died and it is time to recognize it and move on. Positive new beginnings are strongly emphasized with the Judgment card. The card shows you the way to revitalize your life and move into a new phase of higher awareness and purpose.

This is a card of karma - you reap what you sow - what goes around, comes around.

It could literally mean judgment - of yourself or others - are you being too harsh, too critical or negative? Get in touch with the judgmental aspect of yourself and consider whether you have been too hard on yourself or another.

Ask yourself what new phase of your life you could be facing.

21 The World

A naked lady is seen in the middle of a wreath holding two wands and wrapped in a purple scarf. In each corner of the card there are figures (as in The Wheel of Fortune, but they look more mature and knowing).

The World card represents a time of completion, triumph, celebration, and the end of a cycle - success and fulfillment. Awareness has been reached - a moment of completion, and this will be followed by a new cycle. There will be a joyful end and an exciting new beginning to look forward to. Once something is complete and nothing more can be added, it is time to move on. The card represents integration and wholeness on all levels; physical, emotional, mental and spiritual. You now dance life, not just walk through it.

The four mystical creatures represent the four fixed signs of the zodiac. They are the bull (Taurus), lion (Leo), eagle (Scorpio), and man (Aquarius), seen earlier in the Wheel of Fortune. In the Wheel of Fortune they had wings of divine potential, now they are fully realized.

The two wands represent the balance between the material and spiritual realms. Unity is achieved, everything is harmonious and the completion of a cycle is imminent.

The joyful dancer represents our inner Self united. Both feminine and masculine principles have been integrated in our consciousness. We are aware of our place within the universe and we feel in harmony with the world around us.

A time of clarity and clear vision and spiritual enlightenment.

The Minor Arcana - stages of growth
Pentacles

Pentacles represent the element of earth, which is the physical body, which means health and practical matters such as money, family and the home. The suit of Pentacles tends to be quite bright and cheery generally.

Swords

Swords represent the element of air, which is our mental energy, our mind. The mind has great power over us. Swords remind us of how we perceive the world and how we create our dramas in life with our mind. If the mind is calm and peaceful, our outlook on life will follow. If the mind is erratic, then our mental energy will follow, resulting in pain and sorrow.

Wands

Wands represent the element of fire, which is connected to the Spirit. If we have too much fire we have too much heat, which can result in restlessness, being irrational, too energetic, overly confident. If we have too little then this will result in lethargy, lack of self esteem, lack of ambition, lack of creativity and general 'get up and go'.

Cups

Cups represent the element of water, which is linked to our emotions, our feelings. It takes much study to be in control of our emotions and understand the Self. We all aspire to reach the emotional maturity of the Queen and King.

Numbers of minor arcana
The ten opportunities of growth

ACES (ones) - represent fresh energy, the start of something new which carries new potential. Ones indicate that possibly it is soon time to make a decision, time to begin something. An exciting time when the Ace appears as long as the opportunity presented is taken and not ignored.

TWOS - often indicate that a decision will soon be presented to you or possibly a situation with two alternatives. To use a set of scales as a symbolism perfectly represents this number. Two can represent duality such as Yin and Yang, light and dark, male and female, for instance, and the challenge is to unite these energies and recognize the fact that we need both of these opposing forces.

THREES - could be seen as a restless number. It is not a time to sit back and relax, it is time to prepare for action. A time to 'go with the flow'.

FOURS - represent a time to enjoy some stability and enjoy the fruits of past actions. It is knowing when to step back from time to time and when to then get back on the treadmill, ready for the next phase of activity and challenges.

FIVES - Fives can often represent the opportunity to change direction. All four Fives look quite challenging cards. Fives represent the height of a challenge and conflict, and this conflict could be with others or possibly represent inner conflict. This could mean a state of mind that is self-sabotaging and time to take some healing. This time of chaos and frenzy will pass and the challenge is to know when to leave battles behind and move on.

SIXES - Symbolize harmony and balance. When a six energy is around you it is time to be at peace, recognize the journey taken so far and to know that soon it will be time to move on. Six represents relationships, not only with others which could mean partner, friends or family, but also with the Self.

SEVENS - A sign of victory or achievement, seven stimulates an increase in energy, and often new inspiration will come to you and possibly self-realizations. This is a time of movement and development, not a time of peace and tranquility. Also a time to focus, which could be on whatever your particular challenge is at that time, possibly family, relationships, work, etc.

EIGHTS - time to evaluate how we practice balance in our lives whether this applies to work, relationships, money or spirituality. Is too much energy being spent on one energy and not enough on the others? For instance, are you spending too much time trying to make money and focusing entirely on the material side of life and are you neglecting your spiritual side which means time for contemplation, leisure, meditation, healing, etc.?

NINES - this energy indicates you are coming towards the end of your challenge, the end of a particular cycle in your life. A good time to evaluate the situation around you and resolve any issues that are outstanding.

TENS - represent the end of a cycle. Numerologically they are related to ones and share some of the same symbolism. In the Tarot, tens tell of transformations and higher wisdom to be gained, which means learning much from your past experiences. This is an end of a period in your life, coming to the beginning of a new one, and this prepares us for our next spiral of growth.

Court cards - heading to maturity

The following court cards represent periods of growth within the Self. They represent the different stages of maturity that we experience through our lives. They can sometimes also represent a person around you, for instance the Page could represent a child, the Knight a young adult and the King or Queen a mature figure in your life.

PAGES - represent the adolescent stage within the Self. It shows us that at times we act in this way and could represent this inexperienced energy to others, in other words this is how they see you, like a teenager, who think they know it all and have all the answers. You have come through the suit and have gained some wisdom, but you still have further to walk down your path. You have certain control of your feelings and emotions but have yet to mature in this way.

KNIGHTS - represent the early adult stage within the self. You have grown from a child to an adult in the physical body but how do you express yourself, how do you deal with your feelings, have you accepted your responsibilities in life? Knights remind us of virtues such as patience, focusing energy will bring rewards and results; sometimes there is a need to step back and contemplate rather than the 'gung-ho' approach to matters.

QUEENS - represent the female power. Queens have experienced life and have gained control of the emotions and feelings. She offers insight through her intuition and is someone you can go to with your problems to seek guidance. A balanced Queen will use her power in the correct way; she knows and loves herself and understands where she is in life. She could represent a female figure such as Mother, Sister, Wife, etc.

KINGS - represent the male power. Kings often give counsel, as like the Queen they have experienced life and its challenges and people will come to them for guidance and wisdom. Whereas the Queen will offer guidance, the King can sometimes be a little opinionated and will tell you what to do. They could represent a mature male figure such as Father, Brother, Husband, etc.

Summary
Tarot is a great tool for when you reach a crossroads in your life, when your mind is clouded and you need clarity, and for when

you feel you need guidance. There are many people who do Tarot readings who give more of a fortune telling reading. Fortune telling is not spiritual guidance, which means avoiding those readers who will claim to tell you your future. Also, you do not need to be told things you already know, such as you have two children, one brother and three sisters. How can that give you help and guidance?

A good reading can be life-changing and extremely uplifting, so again, use your discernment with your choice of reader and with regards to payment, assess what you think good guidance is worth. Doing readings is time-consuming and can be quite draining so a charge is necessary for the readers for their time and energy.

The Tarot Life Journey

With the Fool, there is no beginning and no end, just as in the cycle of life and death. The Fool will appear at the birth, either of a person or a project or a new stage in life. The Magician will transform the birth into reality, put an idea into action. The High Priestess is the Divine Feminine within the Self, which means your intuition, your nurturing, caring Self-love energy that is often hidden. The Empress is the Mother and The Emperor is the Father, which could mean our own Mother and Father as well as these energies within the Self. For us to be created, we need both of these energies and whatever the circumstances you are born into, your Mother and Father would have joined together to procreate resulting in your life on Earth and the fruits that life has. The Hierophant will remind you that you have free will in life and to not necessarily take on the views of your Parents but to form your own. The Lovers will teach you that there is much to learn from others in the form of relationships, and if you are not in a relationship then be comfortable with the Self. The Chariot will remind you to stay focused in life, enjoy your journey, travel, see the world, meet other people, perhaps have some direction and goals. Strength will teach you to use diplomacy to get what you want in life rather than brute force and ignorance. She also reminds us to keep our own inner strength and power, to not give it away to others. The Hermit shows us that often in life you will need to spend time alone, off the treadmill, find the Self, light up the Soul, connect spiritually and heal the past. If you ignore the Hermit then fate will step in, and The Wheel of Fortune can help you change direction if you are off your path. Justice reminds us that when making big decisions in life to think through the consequences and to not take decisions lightly. The Hanged Man suggests that at times you need to step back, look at things from different angles and to not 'jump out of the frying pan into the fire'. Death can also mean change, something that possibly you are avoiding? Death is a rite of passage that we all go through, whether it is at a crossroads in life or the final death of the physical body. Through life, we shed many skins. Change should not be feared but embraced. After change, there is a chance to re-balance and Temperance can tempt you away from your everyday surroundings to take a break, find some peace and harmony to re-charge your batteries, your energy. Temperance teaches you about moderation which means not too much of something, not too little. The Devil will teach you about blockages and negativity you may be holding onto. The Devil will show you that you are not trapped, you can find liberation from the situation and take control. To remove blocked energy can result in the energy of The Tower; you may feel like your head is exploding, but to release old ways and patterns is liberating and very healing, and to have a spring clean is good not only for the home, but for the emotions, mind and soul. Now you can congratulate yourself and enjoy this beautiful space you are in with The Star. Connecting spiritually will bring peace and harmony. Finding your spirit guides is finding beauty, and The Star will manifest your positive thoughts and wishes. The Moon reminds you of how too much of this energy can result in introspection. If you are in a time of confusion, allow this time and try not to fight and battle with the Self. Meditation can bring clarity and Self-realizations, and this is a time to just be, not to make rash decisions. Then the bright Sun appears and you start to see some light. After the introversion of the Moon period, now is a time for energy and elation, expanding outwards. Judgment teaches us that cycles are natural and there are ups and downs in life. Perhaps time to move into a new phase and feel this new energy. Hopefully you will have learned from past challenges and possible mistakes and not keep repeating patterns. Karma is the fruits of past actions and those fruits can be sweet or sour. The World represents completeness and wholeness. You have completed a cycle in your life, you will have learned from your lessons and challenges and the tyrants presented to you, and you will have gained inner growth and wisdom. You know what contentment, joy and happiness are and you are ready to walk further down your path.

Chapter 8

Aromatherapy

Aromatherapy is the use of essential oils to promote health and well-being. The oils are extracted from plants - leaves, flowers, trees, berries, fruits, resins, etc. The most commonly used method of Aromatherapy is body massage. This is a wonderful, relaxing and healing therapy. The oils are blended to suit your needs and the Therapist will massage the oils on your body, often including the face and scalp. A thorough treatment will take well over an hour, often an hour and a half. As you lie on the treatment couch you will not only receive the therapeutic benefits of the oils used but the massage touch is also very healing and is a lovely tactile treatment. An Aromatherapy Massage will relieve any stress you may have physically, emotionally and mentally.

For massage, essential oils must be blended with a base oil (i.e.: grapeseed oil, almond oil, etc.) but other ways of using aromatherapy oils are adding a few neat drops to your bath, burning the oils in water in a proper oil burner which gives off an aroma, in creams and skin and hair care products, in steam inhalations, a few drops on your pillow to help you sleep, or compresses - put a few drops of the appropriate oil onto a compress or a flannel and press on the area of the body. You could also make your own air freshener by placing some water in a spray bottle with a few drops of glycerin for preservation, and then add a few drops of a pleasing aromatherapy oil such as Rose and Patchouli.

Hand Massage on Yourself or Another
1) Rub oil all over hands and down arms.
2) Using your thumbs, rub across back of hand and work

down line of fingers, from knuckle down towards wrist.

3) Circle each finger and rub from bottom towards tip, slowly.
4) Massage around wrist and thumb-massage down arm towards elbow, 3 times.
5) Turn hand around and work on palm and thumb joint.
6) Massage down arm towards elbow, 3 times.
7) Thumb-massage each finger from bottom to top.
8) Hold hand between your own hands to finish.

Face Massage

A recommended facial oil blend would be Rose and Frankincense.

1) Rub oil into both hands and using upward movements cover neck and face with oil.
2) Using upward movements, massage neck and under chin area, 10 times.
3) Using thumb and middle finger, pinch along jaw line from middle outwards.
4) Trace jaw line, 4 times.
5) Using finger tips and working from middle outwards, massage chin to ears, top of lips to ears, trace cheek bones to ears, and across forehead to temples.
6) Using ring finger, press on third eye and hold for 8 seconds.
7) Using ring finger, circle around eyes, 6 times.
8) Press pressure points - across forehead, under cheek bones.
9) Repeat number 5.
10) Using upward sweeping movements, massage whole face and chin to finish.

For 30ml of base oil you will need 10 drops of essential oil. For

Your Quest For Spiritual Knowledge

a child or for use during pregnancy blend 3-5 drops of essential oil. It is advisable to do skin tests first as some allergic reaction may occur to the skin.

Most commonly used essential oils

Lavender - A good oil for most conditions. Very relaxing oil, good for calming stressful situations, relaxes muscles. Excellent for headaches, skin conditions and infection of the lungs. Put a few drops neat on insect bites and stings and minor burns. Put a few drops on your pillow to help you sleep.

Geranium - A very balancing oil. Balances hormones, very feminine floral aroma. Good for skin problems and is both uplifting, so good for depression, and also a sedative, so good for calming nervous system.

Frankincense - Good one to burn when doing meditation. Frankincense is a very calming oil. It is good for coughs and colds and is emotionally calming.

Neroli - Orange blossom flower has a beautiful aroma. It is very uplifting emotionally and is good for lifting spirits. It is also good for PMT.

Rosemary - A very herby aroma. It is a good stimulant, especially for circulation and mentally. It helps with scalp problems. Rosemary is also good for respiratory conditions. It warms the muscles, so good for muscle tension and spasms.

Rose - A very uplifting floral aroma which is a good mood enhancer. It is used for menstrual problems. Rose is good for skincare and is often used in facial and body creams. It is uplifting emotionally and mentally. Rose has a beautiful aroma.

Tea Tree - A good oil to have in your first aid kit along with Lavender. It is good for insect bites and stings. Tea Tree is an antiseptic oil which is also anti-fungal and anti-bacterial so good for cleaning minor cuts and wounds and grazes. It is used to get rid of warts and verrucas and is useful as an insect repellent.

Chamomile - A very calming oil which is suitable for use on

children along with Lavender. It is good for any situation which requires calming and de-stressing. Chamomile is good for indigestion, rheumatism, menstrual problems, etc. It helps with insomnia as it is generally relaxing.

Orange - A refreshing but sedative oil, orange is a tonic for anxiety and depression. It is good for constipation and stimulates the digestive system. Orange is an uplifting oil. It is known to help reduce stretch marks during pregnancy.

Patchouli - An earthy aroma which you will either love or hate. It is excellent for grounding your energies and is beautiful when blended with Rose.

Clary Sage - A great oil for getting clarity on a situation and having a clear mind in general. Excellent for burning, especially when the mind needs to be focused.

Black Pepper - A really warming oil and is good for relaxing tense muscles. Nice to blend with Lavender.

Eucalyptus - Excellent for clearing the head and nasal passages, especially if blocked with a cold.

Ylang Ylang - Lovely to burn with Eucalyptus for a fresh aroma in the room. Emotionally it is uplifting and will refresh your mind.

Head Lice

An excellent blend of 3-4 drops of the following oils in a palmful of shampoo would be Rosemary, Lavender, Eucalyptus and Geranium. Simply wet the hair, rub the oils and shampoo together in the palms of your hands, massage into the scalp and all over the hair. Leave on for 10 minutes and then rinse off. Repeat this process three days later and then one week later. This is a harmless method of getting rid of head lice and is excellent for the scalp and hair at the same time!

Colds and blocked nose

Place six drops of Lavender and six drops of Eucalyptus in a large bowl of freshly boiled water. Lean over the bowl and place a towel covering your head and the bowl. Inhale deeply. Feel the instant relief from a blocked nose. Do this 2-3 times a day when you have a cold.

Clarity of Mind
Burn 3-4 drops of Clary Sage in a burner.

Relaxing Bath
Run the bath water and at the end place 3-4 drops each of Lavender, Rosemary and Black Pepper in the water. Swish the oil around with your hand. Jump in and let the oils relax your tense muscles.

For an emotionally lifting bath, place 5 drops of Neroli and 3 drops of Geranium into the water.

If you have a cold, place 5 drops of Eucalyptus and 3 drops of Rosemary into your bath water. As above, swish around. Jump in and inhale and exhale deeply.

Room Spray
Place water in a spray container and a few drops of glycerin to preserve your blend. Place 10-15 drops each of Rose and 5 drops of Patchouli into the container and give the blend a good shake with the lid on. Spray around the room for a beautiful fresh aroma. Also excellent for smelly pet beds.

Relaxing Massage blend
Pour a base oil such as sweet almond into a 30ml container. Add 5 drops of Chamomile and 5 drops of Lavender to the base oil and give a good shake with the lid on.

Sensual Massage blend
Pour a base oil into a 30ml container and add 5 drops of Rose and 5 drops of Patchouli. Give the blend a good shake with the lid on.

Muscle Relaxant

Pour a base oil into a 30ml container. Add 3 drops of Rosemary, 3 drops of Lavender and 4 drops of Black Pepper to the container. Shake before use.

Itchy Skin

Try a very small patch first and do a skin test. To relive itchy skin pour some base oil into a small dish or bowl. Add 10 drops of German Chamomile and 5 drops of Lavender and swish around with your finger to blend. Apply to itchy skin, being aware that the oil may stain clothes.

Laundry

Eco-friendly laundry products can sometimes be a little bland. Try adding a few drops of your favorite oil to the washing powder as you place in washing machine.

Make your own laundry spray as for 'Room Spray' with something refreshing like Lavender and Geranium and spray your bed sheets and pillows, etc.

Anti-depressant

Use uplifting, refreshing oils like Neroli, Rose and Ylang Ylang. Blend your own room spray and burn these oils in a burner to keep the energy uplifted.

Skin Care Products

The most natural products to use on your skin are those that have ingredients derived from nature. Many skincare products contain chemicals and these potentially harmful chemicals will be absorbed through your skin and into your body, albeit in minimal amounts, but these chemicals can build up and unless your body can eliminate these toxins, disease may occur. Try to use natural, organic products that will be kinder to the environment in the production and to you as you apply these creams and lotions to your skin. Avoid products that have preservatives such as Parabens which can cause allergic reactions. Natural preservatives are rose or propolis extract. AHA's stand for 'alpha hydroxy acids' and these are used in anti-ageing products. Concentrated AHA's are lactic or glycolic acid and this gives the skin a smoother appearance. I think the word 'acid' says it all!

Alcohol is in many skin products and for some sensitive folk, this will feel like the skin is burning as it is applied, which it probably is.

Check all labels to make sure the products are not tested on animals.

Beauty comes from the inside, not from line-free skin. It is madness to pump chemicals such as Botox into your skin to make you look younger. What harm is this doing to your body and organs long-term?

Chapter 9

.

Crystals

Crystals are gifts from Mother Earth; they are stones comprising natural minerals and are sourced from the ground. Mother Earth has provided these beautiful stones for us to use in healing. Like all things, crystals are made up of energy. This energy emanates healing rays which are absorbed into our bodies to heal the physical body, the emotions and the mind. If you hold a crystal in your hand you may feel this energy in the form of heat or a vibration. Crystals come in the most amazing variety of colors, shapes and sizes. As with the Tarot, you choose the one that you are drawn to, as this is your intuition guiding you as to which crystal you need at that moment, which healing energies you need from that particular crystal. Some crystals give off grounding energies, some connect to spiritual energies, some will direct energy to a Chakra within yourself, some will absorb the negativity from you or the environment.

After you have purchased your crystal you will need to cleanse it, to re-charge it and, if you use if often, then follow this process regularly. Most crystals can be cleansed in running water, ideally a river or stream. Exceptions to this are crystals like Selenite, Celestite and a few others - refer to a crystal book for more information. Sunlight will also cleanse your crystal, so place in the bright sunlight for several hours. Moonlight is another cleanser, so place your crystal on a window sill or ideally outside in the garden overnight on a full moon.

When meditating, place the crystal in your hand or on your lap, or surround yourself with several stones, for instance several pieces of Amethyst. Also, you can place a crystal or several crystals upon your body, for instance as you lie down, place amethyst on your brow chakra or citrine on your solar plexus chakra.

Place crystals around the house, following your intuition as to where you think they should be placed. Place gentle, soothing crystals such as Amethyst or Rose Quartz under your pillow to aid restful sleep.

Crystals can also be worn as jewelry. While you are wearing them, they will be sending out healing energies to you. Jewelry is a good way of knowing that you will be protected from others' energies, especially if you are in the company of people who will drain your energy.

Amethyst

Amethyst is a stunning purple color and comes in different shades. It helps with meditation because it will help you to focus as it calms the mind, the mental energy.

Place in your hand while meditating. Amethyst has strong healing and cleansing powers and enhances spiritual awareness. It alleviates stress, dispels anger, fear and

anxiety, and is emotionally healing. Spiritually, it is a protective stone. It balances the hormone system. As it heals the brow chakra, it eases headaches and reduces tension.

Aventurine

Aventurine is a gentle, pale green. It protects against environmental pollution, so can be worn in jewelry or carried around in your pocket. It is good at dispelling negative energy, therefore it is good for protection, especially if you are sensitive to others' energies and feel you take on their negativity, or you feel that someone is draining your energy. It protects the heart chakra, so you can still have empathy and compassion for others but you are not actually taking on their 'stuff'. It benefits the thymus gland and balances blood pressure, so is good for alleviating stress. It also relieves skin problems, which are often stress-related.

Aquamarine

Aquamarine is a calming, pale aqua blue. It brings peace to the mind and helps you to relax. It is a stone of courage. Its calming energies reduce stress and quieten the whole self.

It has the power to invoke tolerance of others. Spiritually, it sharpens intuition and encourages clairvoyance and increases awareness. It also shields the aura, which is useful when engaging in psychic work. It heals the throat chakra and therefore is useful for sore throats, swollen glands and thyroid problems. It calms autoimmune diseases such as hay fever.

Blue Lace Agate

Blue lace agate is a soft, cooling and calming stone which brings peace of mind. It is good for healing and activating the throat chakra. It counteracts mental stress by cooling the energy down, bringing peace and serenity. Emotionally,

the peaceful energies neutralize feelings of anger. It releases shoulder and neck tension and generally strengthens the skeletal system.

Carnelian

Carnelian is a balancing orange. It heals and removes blockages from the sacral chakra, which is one of the grounding centers. It earths and anchors you in the present reality. As the sacral chakra is where the energy of creativity is, by clearing the blockages creativity will be stimulated. We all have creativity in some form, but it is whether this energy can be expressed. Carnelian helps with life choices, it motivates for success. The lower back is known to be the place of our supporting energy, and this area will be strengthened. It tunes daydreamers in to everyday reality. It dispels mental lethargy.

Citrine - yellow

Citrine is a powerful cleanser and regenerator. It is warming and energizing. It is particularly good for the solar plexus, the fire center relating to our ego. It is useful for smoothing family discord, so if family issues need healing, then place citrine around the home. It raises self-esteem and improves self-motivation. Mentally, it enhancesconcentration and revitalizes the mind. Emotionally, it promotes joy in life. Being a solar plexus healing crystal, it heals digestive problems. Often digestive problems stem from anxiety and stress, so this stone will help with this. Place on the stomach area during meditation.

Clear Quartz

If you feel you aren't getting anywhere with your meditation, try holding a piece of clear quartz. It will open up your crown chakra, connecting you with the Divine. It is a very powerful healing and energy amplifier. It absorbs, stores, releases and regulates energy, and is excellent for unblocking it. It is very cleansing to organs and the subtle body, and acts as a deep soul cleanser. Quartz is a master healer as it stimulates the immune system and brings the body into balance. It harmonizes all chakras.

Hematite

If you find that when meditating you drift off into another world and find it difficult coming back, then hematite is the crystal for you. Hold it in your hands and also place it on your feet while meditating. It is very grounding and will keep you earthed. It also offers protection, preventing negative energies from entering your aura, which is helpful if you are sensitive to others' energy. It is vital that you look after your own life force and be aware that there are people out there who unintentionally will drain your energy. This crystal is a very dark gray and is often polished so it looks appealing, hence it is often found in necklaces and bracelets. Hematite is really good to wear in jewelry as it harmonizes the mind, body and spirit. It is known to boost your self-esteem . It is useful for overcoming addictions when used with other therapies. It aids circulatory problems and is good for insomnia if placed under the pillow at night.

Jasper

Jasper is a stunning earthy color and comes in different shades of orangey, browny red. It is another very grounding stone and can be placed around the body while meditating. It particularly heals the sacral chakra and base chakra if these centers are blocked. It will free fear, anger, life blockages i.e.: being 'stuck in a rut' and is an excellent healer for the lower back. Lie on your tummy with Jasper placed on your lower back. It provides protection and grounds energies and the body. It absorbs negative energies and re-aligns the chakras. It is known to facilitate shamanic journeys and dream recall. It can bring courage as the lower chakras are unblocked. It supports the sexual organs and is very healing if placed on the ovary area while lying down to ease menstrual cramps.

Lapis Lazuli

Lapis Lazuli is the most gorgeous blue color with gold flecks. It is often sourced from Egypt, where of course the ancient Egyptians would have powdered it to make their stunning blue eye makeup. It opens the third eye, so will aid visions and enhance psychic abilities. It is a strong healer for the throat chakra, so will balance the thyroid and clear any blockages in this center, which is useful if you suffer with sore throats. Lapis Lazuli will enhance dreams. It releases stress, bringing peace. It helps you to confront truth and take charge in life as the more your throat chakra is cleared, the easier it will be to express yourself. It alleviates pain, especially migraine headaches. As it brings peace, it helps to overcome depression and benefits the respiratory and nervous systems. It alleviates insomnia, promotes feelings of peace and it lowers blood pressure.

Malachite

Malachite is a beautiful deep green containing dark bands and rosettes and is really appealing to the eye. Malachite is known to have extremely strong powers. These energies are very protective and it is ideally worn as a pendant protecting the heart and chest area, as it absorbs negative energy. It will heal the heart chakra, opening you up to unconditional love. Malachite will help you to connect with your Spirit Guides, and if you state this intention during meditation this link will develop. It is often said that this is not the stone for beginners and should only be used when you have a little experience of working with energies. The dust is toxic, so it is best used in the polished form.

Moldavite

Moldavite is a dark green, transparent, often glassy crystal which is quite expensive because of its rarity. It is known as a 'New Age' crystal as it is said to have extraterrestrial origin, formed when a giant meteorite struck the earth. Some people (often known as The Star People, who are here to increase the vibration) have the belief that there are other intelligent races to connect to on a different planet, and for them this is the stone to work with. It is used to work with 'higher energies' such as Ascended Masters and to receive cosmic messages, so is excellent in meditation. This is not the stone for ungrounded people! Moldavite will align the chakras and will enhance the energies of your other crystals.

Moonstone

A beautiful feminine, blue crystal with almost a hint of pink. It helps with anything Yin / Moon; in other words the divine feminine energies within, in particular the emotions. It will help to balance the emotions and is ideally worn in a pendant over the heart and chest area and will also help with any emotionally-linked issues such as asthma, hay-fever, digestive problems, etc., as it is really calming. It is excellent for any female physical issues such as PMT, ovary problems and during menstruation. With the Moon cycle being the same length of time as the female menstrual cycle of 28 days, it is powerful for tuning into your emotions and feelings. For men it would be ideal for bringing out their feminine side.

Obsidian Black

If you are drawn to Black Obsidian then it is likely you are ready to do some deep Soul work. It will ground spiritual energies and give you focus, helping you to learn about the true Self; the Soul. When Soul searching, your Moon energies will emerge; these energies are your cooler energy, your darker self. This doesn't mean to say that you are a mean killer but simply means that you may have hidden emotions, suppressed anger or unrecognized patterns that you are stuck in. Black Obsidian, when used during your Soul searching and healing process, will unblock energies and help you with this transformational process, so you can walk your spiritual path in peace and harmony.

Rose Quartz

Rose Quartz is a soft pink and just emanates peace and love. It is known as the stone of unconditional love and infinite peace. It is the most important crystal for the heart and the heart chakra. It gently replaces negative energy with loving vibes. It aids the acceptance of necessary change that we so often resist. It will open your heart to receive love. As it heals the emotions and brings you peace, it aids chest and lung problems. It is used a lot in jewelry, and pieces of rose quartz can be placed around the home and beside the bed to aid restful, peaceful sleep.

Sodalite

Sodalite is a deep blue with very dark veins running through it. It has very similar qualities to Lapis Lazuli but is known as the 'poor man's version'. It clears blockages at the throat chakra and therefore instills a drive for truth, clearing communication blockages. It enhances meditation as it stimulates the third eye, the center of seeing. It clears electromagnetic pollution, so is useful placed in the office or around the home. It is an excellent stone for the mind as it eliminates mental confusion and brings clarity. It balances the metabolism as it helps to balance the thyroid and cleanses the lymphatic system and organs, boosting the immune system. As it treats the throat, it keeps the vocal cords and larynx healthy. Sodalite cools fevers and lowers blood pressure, so is good for someone with too much fire energy.

Tiger's Eye

Tiger's Eye is a beautiful, earthy brown with golden brown stripes, and is very appealing to the eye. It has grounding energies and is used to heal the base chakra. It is a protective stone, so is good to use in psychic work if you are sensitive to energies. It balances the lower chakras; the base especially, the sacral and the solar plexus, so is useful in healing if you have your 'head in the clouds' and need to connect with your earthing energies. As these centers are linked to energies such as fear, ambition, direction and goals, it assists in accomplishing these goals by helping you to stay centered and focused. When placed on the sacral chakra, it is excellent for people who are spaced out and need grounding. Also it heals mental disease and personality disorders. Tiger's eye alleviates depression and lifts moods. It treats the eyes and aids night vision and heals physical problems related to the lower chakras such as the reproductive organs, back issues, etc.

Once the lower chakras are cleared, the kundalini energy can rise.

Chakras and Crystals

The following diagram shows the positions of the seven main chakras, and listed below are suggestions of crystals which may be used in working with and healing these chakras.

Base Chakra – Tiger's Eye, Hematite
Sacral Chakra - Carnelian, Jasper
Solar Plexus - Yellow Citrine
Heart - Rose Quartz, Aventurine, Malachite
Throat - Lapis Lazuli, Sodalite
Brow - Amethyst, Lapis Lazuli
Crown - Clear Quartz

Chapter 10

Shamanism

Shamanism is simply being connected to Earth energies, which means to nature, being grounded, feeling linked to Mother Earth, as well as being connected to The Great Divine, to Spirit energies.

Generations ago, every village would have had a Shaman; someone who would have provided medicine from herbs and plants grown around them, someone who would have given healing to those who were in need, which means healing channeled from Spirit. Shamans would have provided divination to those who wanted insight. Shamans have always existed, and the traditions have been kept going in certain cultures like the Siberians, Native American Indians and the Incas of Peru. Their methods vary, but the essence of respecting Mother Earth and linking to Spirit remains the same for all. At the present time there are more and more Shamanic Practitioners being trained, which is perhaps what is needed. Shamanic Practitioners can reach the Soul in a more direct and effective way.

Shamanic healing differs from other forms of healing such as Reiki, as the energy is different. If you have experienced Angel Healing or Reiki Healing, although the energy is beautiful and has its own value, it is much more subtle compared to that of Shamanic healing which seems to be much more direct, to the point, rather like drilling with a pneumatic drill - very powerful and effective!

My experience is that energy healing such as Reiki is a beautiful therapy but is fairly subtle, whereas Shamanic Healing works at a Soul level; at a much deeper level.

The Medicine Circle and The Four Directions

The four directions are used as a healing tool within the sacred circle. This method has been used by indigenous peoples all over the world and is still used today by people such as the Native Americans and the Aborigines and also by Shamanic Practitioners all over the world. The Medicine Circle is a multi-layered map of the universe and in these maps you will find what direction to take. Within the circle are aspects of human beings and the challenge for us all is to find the real knowledge and separate it from the 'false teachings' that we have had imprinted on our minds as we grow up in society. Each direction has a relation to a cardinal point, an element, a totem animal, a season, a place of healing, and dark and light energies. The healing process involves passing through each direction, round the circle. It is believed that we travel round and round this healing circle as we journey through life. As we journey through life we meet our challenges, and hopefully learn from them and evolve into an enlightened stage of peace, harmony and balance.

North - air - mind - everyday adult - clarity - wisdom - winter - Jaguar

The north is correlated to our mind, our mental energy. These are the qualities of the suit of Swords in the Tarot. The mind has great power over us. Our mind dictates how we perceive the world and how we create our dramas in life. If the mind is calm and peaceful, our outlook on life will follow. If the mind is erratic, then our mental energy will follow, resulting in pain and sorrow. In today's world our minds are often full of nonsense, causing us stress and distress. Life can be chaotic in the modern world and therefore our minds are chaotic, causing an unhealthy body. If the mind is calm, peaceful and in balance then the body will follow. Winter is a time of retreat, introspection, darkness, cold, and sometimes chaos needs to be experienced in order to experience clarity. Winter is a time that should be embraced and enjoyed by taking more time indoors and using this time to relax, read, do crafts, cook, sit in front of the fire, etc.

Our challenge is to separate real knowledge from the 'false knowledge', in other words to seek The Higher Truth.

Meditation will calm the mind, and the North is a time to work with this mental energy.

South - water - emotions - inner child - fear - trust and innocence- healing wounds - summer - Mouse

In the South is where we heal the emotional body. As children we cannot control the emotions and this is learned as we go into adolescence. By adulthood one would hope that we have learned how to express ourselves and control outbursts and reactions to situations. The South helps to heal the emotional body and teaches us how to deal with our emotions. Fear can be replaced with trust. This will require opening up past wounds that the memory has very cleverly stored away and tried to shut the door on. Also, we store emotions in cells of the body, which is known as cellular memory. This is why through stretching the muscles in practices such as Yoga, emotional tension is released, albeit on a subtle level. Shamanic healing will drill down to the wound, pull it out, then deep healing and transformation can take place. When we heal our wounds, we heal the wounds of our Ancestors, our lineage.

East - Fire - Spirit - freedom - enlightenment - power - spring - Eagle

The East is where the sun rises each day, bringing light into the world. Through connecting to Spirit, we find our freedom and realize our true power. This is like a new beginning. The East is where we will see visions, see the Self, get to know the real you. This new beginning can only be made if there is a conscious effort and a choice made to want to heal. In order to walk the spiritual path, the wounds have to be healed. You can then become a clearer channel. It is life shedding a load. The choice is yours! You can be empowered by healing your wounds, become Master of your Self. Be the Majical Child!

West - earth - physical body - inner Goddess - death - introspection - autumn - Bear

Autumn is a preparation time for winter. The West energy is change and death, experiences that we make great dramas out of. Most people resist change instead of embracing it, making the challenge far more difficult. A lot of people have a great fear of death and this is something that can be erased once this deep healing process takes place and blocked energy is shifted and a connection with Spirit is made. You will understand that while we don't wish our loved ones to die, death is nothing to fear as the Spirit World is another vibration which is all around us, closer than you may possibly be thinking. Shift your blocked energy of fear by Meditation and Dance.

The Center - Elder - Wisdom

To be in the space of the center is to walk in your own power, to love life, to feel joy and happiness, to take full responsibility, to feel light and be in harmony with the world.

Smudging

Smudging is where the smoke from a burning smudge stick made up of herbs such as sage and lavender, along with a feather, is used to cleanse your aura, to bring you into the present, to put you into a sacred space.

You can smudge yourself or someone else can smudge your aura for you, which is more effective as they can reach right around the back of your body.

Rooms can also be smudged, and even whole buildings, to clear energy and again create a sacred space ready for you to do your 'energy work'.

The Drum

Along with the rattle, the drum is a powerful healing tool. The continuous beat carries a vibration with the sound. The drum is used in Journeying, Trance Dance and other ceremonies in Shamanism. Indigenous people across the world use the drum in many ways for different ceremonies. The drum beat can take you to an altered state of consciousness and is very healing in the way that it can stir up and release emotions whether it is elation, anger, irritation or fear. To be in a circle with several drums being played is an absolutely awesome experience. Drums can be made out of man-made materials or out of animal skin such as horse or deer.

Manmade drums are known as 'Remos' and can be used at any temperature, either in the Sweat Lodge or outside in the elements, whereas an animal skin drum is more sensitive to temperature and care should be taken in terms of heat or cold, dampness, etc. These things will effect the tone of the drum quite dramatically.

The Talking Stick

When sitting in circle, a talking stick is handed around to each person. While the stick is being held, that person is absolutely the only person who is speaking at that time. Once that person is finished, the stick is then handed around to the next one. The rest of the circle really have to use their listening skills.

Journeying

Journeying is a tool used by Shamanic Practitioners. It takes you to a state of mind know as 'lucid dreaming' - a place between being awake and being asleep, a different level of consciousness. The Practitioner can journey on your behalf or they will drum and lead you into a journey which you take yourself. Journeying will help you to 'see'. You will journey in your psyche. In your journey you may experience meeting your Spirit Guides, your Power Animals, your Ancestors, you may get visions of past, present and future, you may get guidance on an issue. As we live our lives we gather baggage, emotional and mental, which can result in blocked energy in the body, often manifesting into an illness, pain or disease. By healing at a spiritual level, this will help to clear this blocked energy, which will result in a healthy mind, body and spirit. Therefore connection to the true Self, the Soul, takes place as this healing works at this level.

Before you actually take your journey you state the intention; i.e.: 'I journey to the Lower World to meet my Power Animals' or 'I journey to the Lower World to follow the ancestral line of my Father / Mother, to understand the gifts and freedoms as well as the limitations or burdens'.

You can also journey on many different intentions and to seek guidance.

The stages of Journeying are as follows:

* Smudge
* Sit or lie down in a comfortable position
* Relaxation, let the whole body relax
* In your mind, find a sacred place out in nature, for instance out in the countryside or up a mountain
* State the intention of your Journey
* Find an opening into the Earth like a hollowed-out tree, a tunnel going down
* Let the drum take you on your Journey (approximately 10-20 minutes)
* The drum will call you back, prepare
* Come back up the same way you went down
* Find yourself back to the place in nature where you started
* Slowly bring your awareness back

There are three 'places' to journey to. The Lower World will give you your connection to nature and physically relates to your lower Chakras, below the Heart. The Sacral Chakra is a place where we hold deep emotions and wounds. The Middle World is everyday reality, and instead of going down into the Earth as for the Lower World you would enter a gate, or two pillars, or two trees. The Upper World is connecting to your spiritual chakras from the heart above. This is where you would seek guidance 'from above'. Often this is where you would connect to your Spirit Guide and Helpers to seek help on an issue.

Soul Retrieval

This is a tool that is so beneficial for us in today's world. As we journey through our lives, we go through the different rites of passage such as puberty, marriage, becoming parents, experiencing life and death and entering the older, wiser years. We have our challenges, which can be both gifts as well as burdens. We are here to learn from these challenges, to gain wisdom, to not repeat patterns, but often we gather blocked energy in the form of emotional and mental baggage which can then manifest into physical baggage in the form of aches, pains, illnesses and diseases. Through the traumas and incidents we experience in life, we 'lose' some of our life force, a part of our soul. The Shamanic Soul Retrieval will bring back this lost life force and will enable the healing to take place at a soul level.

Often this form of Journeying will be done on your behalf by the Practitioner who will journey for you, find the object of the lost energy and blow the life force back into your body. An example of Soul loss would be being bullied at school, abuse, an accident or trauma, or the loss of a loved one. It is also worth mentioning that these experiences may not necessarily be traumatic; it could be something that occurred which may now seem rather trivial but at the time energy was lost.

Sometimes the Practitioner will drum as you journey with your intention for yourself. An example of this would be you journeying as you are today to a childhood incident where life force was lost, such as a death in the family or could be something more simple like the loss of a favorite toy. This life force would be brought back and then blown back into the body by the Practitioner.

Soul theft is where someone, quite often unintentionally, takes your energy, or where you have given away your power to someone else. Examples of when soul theft can occur are looking up to someone and idolizing them, or down at someone thinking you have more power than them, hatred, wanting someone to change, envy, jealousy, being overly caring, and neediness.

Trance Dance

To the sound of the drum the dancer will pick up the rhythm and move to the beat. Sometimes the dancer is blindfolded. Spotters are placed around the dancer to avoid collision or injury. After a period of time the dancer will connect with Spirit and go into a trance-like state. In this state, there will be a trace of consciousness. At the same time the mind will be concentrated, there will be no outside distractions, just pure Spiritual connection. This is where often power animals come to us in the form of a vision and often the dancer can take on the energy of this animal, which means the dancer could become a dancing, prancing, happy, joyful butterfly, or a mean, vicious, aggressive feline. Deep healing will take place, emotions are released and the transformation of energy will happen, leading to the removal of blocked energy. After the dance, rest is needed, awareness of reality can take a little while, recovery time is essential and much water is needed to help shift energy.

My own personal experience after a trance dance five day workshop was one of deep healing, an incredible shift of blocked energy and emotions that I had been holding on to for years. I felt so cleansed and alive, rejuvenated.

The Sweat Lodge

The Sweat Lodge is seen as the womb of Mother Earth. The ceremony is one of rebirth and renewal. Connection to the four elements and four cardinal directions takes place in a ceremony.

The lodge is often a dome shaped structure built with care and respect to the environment. It is often covered with tarpaulin to bring complete darkness inside. The door faces the external fire. Inside the lodge is a central pit where hot stones which have been heated on the external fire are brought in by the Fire Keeper. A ceremony is performed by the Leader, prayers will be made for yourself and others, there will be drumming and chanting and offerings given to Spirit. The Sweat Lodge is very purifying, which brings insight, self-realizations and wisdom. Deep cleansing takes place.

The Vision Quest

This is where you would go off to a secluded place in nature alone. No food is taken over this period which is normally for a few days minimum, only water for survival. In the Native American tradition the vision quest would be taken at puberty, coming into adulthood. By being alone in the wilderness with no distractions, Spirit comes to offer guidance and give helpful visions. A feeling of being connected to the Spirit of nature will be experienced, possibly seeing beings of nature. The visions may be in the form of Power Animals.

Power Animals

It is believed that all animals have their own healing medicine and healing energies, also bringing guidance as we Journey. These animals bring different qualities such as transformation, protection, calmness, power, teaching or vision. The animal brings the energies you need at that time. Often you find if you are particularly drawn to a certain animal it is because it is that energy that you need to work with.

Power Animals are often seen as Spirit Guides and I find that most people can easily connect to their Power Animal but not so easily to other forms of Spirit Guides like lost loved ones or human energy forms. To take on the energy of an animal can be a form of shape shifting. This is where your mind is totally focused on an animal, your body will take on the form i.e.: your arms may become the wings of a Crow, your voice may screech like a Hawk, your hands become the claws of a Panther. This will help you in instances where you may need, for instance, the courage of a Lion or the ability to see fine details like a Mouse. You can carry the power of the spirit of the animal.

To connect to your Power Animal

Sit quietly and take time to relax. Play some drumming music in the background. Follow the above Journeying procedure going in with the intention of finding your Power Animal. When you have connected to your animal, commune, ask for guidance either in this journey or next time you journey. Come back when you feel ready. This should take around 15-20 minutes.

Trust what you are seeing and don't let the ego dictate and pre-determine your Power Animal. Your ego may be telling you to see an Eagle but your true self may need you to see a mouse! That is because it is the mouse energy that you need at this moment for your development and evolution.

Snake

The Snake is the symbol of transformation. It transforms by shedding its old skin. When this animal comes to you then perhaps you should allow a time of change to take place. Let the transformation of healing happen, release old energy and allow fresh new energy to come to you.

Cat family

You may have a gentle, domestic type cat or a wild, black, vicious panther. Cats, whether domestic or wild, can be extremely vicious; they are very good at standing their ground, getting their claws out ready for the attack. They can go from curling up in front of the fire purring loudly, to being the most aggressive animal. Maybe this is what you need to do in a certain situation in your life; stand your ground. Maybe Cat can help you fight your corner. Panthers and Tigers often appear when protection is needed.

Dog

Dogs are just so loyal. They are always pleased to see their owner, their tails wagging when they arrive home. To the person who walks, feeds and love them, they would give their life up for them. Perhaps this is teaching you about loyalty, maybe how others treat you, with respect and loyalty or maybe the opposite.

Horse

Horses are so gentle considering their size. Man has tamed them over the years and they have served us in many ways. Like all animals they respond to kindness and gentle persuasion rather than brutal controlling power. Their energy is full of courage, wisdom and strength. They are very grounded creatures, literally with four feet on the ground. They can even sleep standing up they are so earthed. The Horse teaches us that you can have size, power and courage, but at the same time a gentle spirit.

Wolf

If you ever have seen the eyes of a wolf close up, the energy that they give is of pure knowing and wisdom. Wolf appears often when we need teaching, in such a way as to awaken our intuition. They are extremely clever animals who follow their instincts and intuition very carefully.

Eagle

When Eagle comes to you it is simply stunning. Eagles fly very high and have incredible vision. They can spot prey from a huge distance, they remain extremely focused and then they will go for the kill. Eagle energy is giving you guidance on seeing something from a higher perspective, seeing the bigger picture. Maybe you are caught up in minute details and missing the point on something. Perhaps your Crown Chakra is awakening, connecting you to your higher self.

Mouse

Mouse energy is almost the opposite to Eagle. Mouse is a little earth animal who skits about, not missing a thing. Perhaps this time, you need to look at the finer details on something that you may have overlooked.

Crow family

The menacing-looking black crow family can be both fierce and adaptable when needed. Like all birds they are messengers; you need to listen to what the message is. They symbolize healing.

Owl

The wise old Owl. Owls have 360 degree vision - they don't miss a trick as they can see all around. They have incredible focus and symbolize knowledge and wisdom. This is not the type of knowledge read in books or through beliefs, this is real knowing. It is that knowing that is gained by reaching your Soul and finding the higher truth.

Swan

Swan is the representation of true beauty and power within yourself. The swan evolves from a duckling with brown feathers to a beautiful creature with grace and serenity. They float across the water with such peace. This energy could be blocked power within yourself that could be awakened, bringing you this peace and liberation.

Geese

Geese are real family animals who stick together. Perhaps this is a time for you to gel with someone in your family and heal some old wounds that could be there with family issues.

Heron

Whereas geese stick together and are found in groups, Heron is often alone and enjoys the solitude. Perhaps this is a time when you would benefit from spending time alone, have a break away, be in solitude for a while, in order for you to grow.

Bat

Bats thrive in darkness and only come out at night. Perhaps this is how you feel - in the dark about something, unknowing regarding a situation or you just feel like you are in this dark energy, blackness, fear, anger, etc. Maybe it is a time to seek some light energy to balance things out.

Bear

The Bear hibernates, going through the depths of winter in the dark in a cave. They are big, powerful animals who are fiercely protective of their young, like most animals. They can really fight and they use their size and strength by rising up on their hind feet, knowing how to use their power. When Bear appears it could be time to go deep within yourself. Bear energy is protective and could be reminding us to look at how we use our power.

Deer

Deer are gentle, timid creatures who roam free in the forest. They show us unconditional love and compassion. They teach us that love is a two-way energy exchange rather than sacrificial. They teach us that in order to get what we want, it takes gentle, persuasive power rather than aggressive, overbearing power. We can learn these things from Deer and bring them into our lives.

Buffalo

The Native Americans would have used every bit of the buffalo; there was no waste. Buffalo shows us that prayers can be manifested and teach us abundance. We sometimes forget that guidance can be sought from Spirit and spend too much time with negativity rather than centering energies, re-connecting to the earth, and re-connecting to Spirit. Buffalo reminds us that everything you need can be sourced.

Elephant

Elephants are gentle giants in their own community. They show true love and stay close in a herd. They are generally slow and can teach us patience. They show emotion when confronted with a dead or dying member of the herd. They embody strength, power and protection. Perhaps these are energies you can learn from.

Dolphin

If you watch dolphins in the wild, they play like children, dancing and jumping in and out of the ocean. They are care-free and send out incredible healing energies. They remind us to be playful at times and to be joyful. Perhaps it is time to get in touch with your inner child; maybe some childhood issues could be raised and transformed.

Lizard

Lizards are earth animals, they bury themselves in the earth. They may be reminding us not to 'bury our head in the sand' when a challenge arises, to face the heat and resolve the problem.

Fox

The fox is sly and cunning and is quite vicious in the way that it will kill as many chickens as it can, but only actually needs one for survival. This can teach us a lot about waste. Fox is a beautiful, clever animal and has a tame, gentle side as well as the other side. Fox can teach us to be diplomatic and to use our cleverness in a positive, creative way rather than a manipulative, cunning way.

Pig

Pigs forage through the forest to find their treasure - the truffles. They can teach us to be patient, keep our head down, to work hard and the rewards will come. They show us that if you use these qualities in your spiritual life then the treasure will be found - your Soul, the essence of who you are.

Rabbit

Rabbits are cute and cuddly but very timid creatures. They show us fear; we all have this energy, and to heal fear we need to confront it and deal with it. At the same time we need to stay grounded and know that fear is sometimes an energy we need to stop us doing dangerous things like jumping off a wall that is far too high with the risk of injury.

Salmon

Wild Salmon make a long and arduous journey to return to their place of creation. This shows sheer determination and shows us that Salmon is in touch with its natural instincts and inner knowing. Salmon has a clear sense of purpose and knows where it is going. These qualities can help you at times when you feel you have no direction, feel out of balance or are confused in your mind. Salmon reminds us to be centered and be in touch with the true Self.

Coyote

Coyote energy is often referred to as child-like, often laughing at our own mistakes. Coyote is known as the trickster, but this is not in a mean way, it is to remind us when we are straying away from our paths. Coyote tells us that we are here to connect to the soul, so when the ego controls us we will get a nudge to remind us why we are here. By connecting to the Soul, you will understand the essence of who you truly are and a balance of earth energies and spiritual energies can be made bringing wisdom, truth and harmony.

Your Quest For Spiritual Knowledge

Chapter 11

Death

When death is imminent, if you are in the presence of someone or something, you can feel the energy changing around their physical body, whether it is a person, animal or even a plant. There is a peaceful energy and you may see a beautiful white light as the Soul and spirit is going home. Of course it is those who are left behind that suffer.

Death is often feared and in modern times we tend to make such a drama out of it. Of course to experience death of your loved ones is a sad, terribly emotional loss, especially if the one who has passed over to Spirit is young, or your own child; a dreadful loss.

When an old person has reached the end of their life it is still very sad, but at least they have experienced life. One hopes that one does not suffer at the end and to die peacefully in sleep must surely be the kindest way. The body can only take a certain amount of pain, then it will shut down, so if a loved one is suffering then ask The Divine, Healing Guides and Angels to relieve the suffering and to send the person healing. This form of healing may help the person to release and pass over to the Spirit World.

Death is a rite of passage, one that we all will take one day. When the last breath is taken on an exhale, the life force will leave the physical body. The physical body becomes perfectly still once all the life force has left. The Soul will pass into the World of Spirit and will be helped along by deceased Ancestors, lost loved ones. This transition takes 9 days and on the 9th day living loves ones often feel sad and this can be a particularly difficult day if they are sensitive. Forty days after the passing, the Soul will be

138

over in the Spirit World and again this can be a difficult day for those sensitive beings and a ceremony such as spreading of the deceased's ashes would be relevant for this day. The essence of the Self, the Soul will come back in another life, to learn more lessons, to find liberation and wholeness. Maybe as a Spiritual Teacher or an evolved Soul who has the right intent, integrity, and works in the most discerning ways, they may not return for another life; this may be the last one. To act in this position without the right intent and integrity, the Soul will definitely return.

The Soul that is whole will ascend to another dimension and will become a Spiritual Guide.

The Spirit World is a place of peace, timelessness and pure light.

Enjoy the fruits of life such as:

Rising to challenges
Enjoying the beautiful countryside and appreciating nature
Tasting and enjoying every mouthful of food
Being with friends and family
Enjoying sex
Exploring other cultures and countries
Career
Seeking the Self
Enjoying the wonderful blessing of being alive on this planet

Count your blessings; appreciate life and the abundance around you.

To be with a person or animal friend as they pass is a beautiful experience and a privilege. To be there, to hold them and help them on their journey. To feel Spirit so close.

When you lose a loved One, give yourself plenty of time for grieving and adjusting. Be in tune with the 9th day and the 40th day of transcending. This is a time for your healing; allow yourself space. Seek counsel if you find it unbearable and nurture yourself in any way that suits your needs.

This healing time is time to allow the transition to occur, the transition of your lost loved One and the transformation of energy within yourself. Let go of your grief, do not hang on to the sad emotion. Your heart chakra will be the center where this energy will be felt, so do plenty of healing on this center.

Chapter 12

Nutrition

There are just too many fad diets out there!

The best advice to give would be to eat food that is right for *your* body and your environment. In terms of right for your body, this will mean eating the right food for your individual needs. For instance, if you are a man who has a physical job such as a Builder then your body will need plenty of protein to give you the energy it needs. If you are a woman who sits down all day in an office, then lighter foods would be more appropriate.

In terms of environment, when it is cold your body will need warm foods such as porridge for breakfast, soup and bread for lunch, and a hot cooked main meal. When it is warm your body will need less food such as muesli for breakfast, fruit and salad for lunch, and a main meal such as protein and salad.

The main points to keep to are as follows:

Keep your diet fairly simple
Eat a balanced diet
Eat what is in season
Be in tune with your body and know what your needs are
Try to eat fresh food. Meat especially starts to putrefy pretty
    quickly
Try to eat organic food if your budget allows (better still,
    grow your own)
Only eat when you are hungry
Include fresh fruit and vegetables in your diet
Cook homemade meals
Drink plenty of water
Avoid:

Sugary foods such as commercial chocolate bars and sweets
and over-sugary desserts

Processed foods

Fizzy drinks

Becoming obsessed with your diet

The following are grounding foods which will help you to
keep earthed:

Meat

Fish

Sugar

Alcohol

Wheat

Dairy products

Caffeine

The following are light foods:

Fresh food

Vegetables

Pulses

Fruit

Water and fruit juices

Assess whether you feel you need to be grounded more or
whether you feel you need to eat lighter foods. For instance,
before meditation or taking any practice involving energy work,
it would be more appropriate to take lighter meals beforehand. If
you are feeling spacey and ungrounded then perhaps eat some
grounding food.

Chapter 13

The Bigger Picture

The Environment

The Planet gives us:

- ~ Fresh water
- ~ Healthy soil
- ~ Breathable air

Respect the planet, the environment, rainforests and oceans. Here are a few tips which all help:

- ~ Be aware of your carbon footprint and how you could reduce it, which could mean cycling or walking instead of using the car, for instance reducing school runs where practical.
- ~ Get your name removed from junk mail databases.
- ~ Reduce usage of plastic.
- ~ Try to buy locally produced food - it makes sense. This applies not only to locally grown produce but also to meat. Avoid meat from poor animals that have suffered long journeys. That energy will be in the food and therefore in your body!
- ~ Recycle - think of things in addition to the normal household waste such as mobile phones, computers, ink cartridges, etc.
- ~ Save power at home - turn off lights, turn appliances right off and not on standby
- ~ When the weather and environment permits, hang washing outside rather than using a dryer, or dry your washing inside the house on an airer.
- ~ With food, only buy what you actually need

~ Spread the word; perhaps join appropriate organisations such as Friends of The Earth.

The Universe

When meditating, spend some time sending loving vibes out to the universe and trust that you are being heard.

Allow yourself a few minutes to relax.

Focus around your heart area.

See a beautiful pink and gold light.

See that light, that energy emanating from your heart, swirling outwards, gradually moving further and further away from your body.

Send out loving thoughts to the Universe.

Just be, in this beautiful space.

Slowly grounding your energies.

Bringing your awareness back.

Use the guidelines above to send out loving, healing vibes to situations that trouble your thoughts such as global warming, war zones, poverty, cruelty to animals, always remembering that you cannot take on the world's troubles; you will probably have enough of your own to deal with. Try to get the balance of being selfless and selfish. Remind yourself that you have your own path and others have theirs.

Manifesting

Every thought you think takes energy into the ether. So if your thoughts are negative such as the world is going to end, poverty makes me feel guilty and ill, the planet is never going to recover, then you are not helping the situation as your thoughts carry energy. If you think of beautiful healthy forests, clean water and fresh air then that is what will manifest; health will be restored to the planet.

Chapter 14

This is an article written by my brother Saemus Corrigan before he tragically died in 1972. (Born 14 September 1951 - 17 February 1972). He was at University studying to be an Architect. This document was discovered when clearing out my late Mother's things in September 2009.

To Explore and Discover my Thinking

I am a very thoughtful person. My mind is always active, always thinking about something or other. I would say that for the most part my thoughts are spontaneous. That is I am usually inspired through circumstances of the moment, for example by reading something in the paper or talking to somebody, watching a film, looking at flowers, trees and other visual stimuli. There are numerous ways in which I am stimulated into thought, employing the use of all my senses. The degree to which I am stimulated is controlled by my sensitivity, that is the value of the impact I receive from the stimuli is controlled by my own individual mind and its particular personality / character make up. The point is that there are good and bad aspects of this way of thinking.

In its favor it means one is always concerned with the present and the future. Reality is the contemplation of now. Of course one might be stimulated to think of what has happened in the past and peruse over past events. But the thinking is done now, it is a question of merely looking out of the back window of a moving car, and not stopping and going back.

But by its very nature of being stimulated by the present thinking can be scattered and inconclusive. The mind may be wandering over some topic when something else suddenly takes an interest. This can be taken to the extreme when several topics are being considered at the same time. This usually results in not much being learned and a tendency for thinking to become established and merely a routine pushing information into the subconscious, usually to be forgotten and never used again. This happens to me occasionally and is disturbing and usually results in depression and apathy. Fortunately these bouts are not very frequent but nevertheless they are important. This makes for inefficient use of input and generally a waste of time. Since time is life it is desirable that I make the most of it, and since thinking is an integrated part of my happiness it is desirable that the utmost efficiency is obtained, that my mind interprets and draws conclusions which are not clouded and vague. The knowledge of certainty is very important to me, I feel I must know.

Obviously it appears that I could benefit from having some sort of organized control over my thought process. Something to follow as a natural sequence of conclusions, a basis from which proper and absolute efficiency can be obtained in contemplation. But I am not aware of such a system and looking for one would defeat the purpose of living. Logic is already under question as the ultimate truth in thinking. People with the same problem as me are finding new ways of looking at things so perhaps somebody will inspire me to change my ways, perhaps not.

I have explored my thinking and even my road to happiness so what have I learned? Well perhaps that my thinking could be improved upon if I am to fulfill my aims in living. The ultimate in thinking for me would be relaxed efficiency, the peaceful contemplation and explorations of life. So at least this project has inspired me to think, and perhaps more important, to continue in my research.

References in *Your Quest for Spiritual Knowledge - The Bhagavad Gita* - Juan Mascaro

Summary of Two Thousand and Twelve and Beyond

This book has been channeled by my Spirit Guides, also using my knowledge gained through study and experience.

The message is clear, which is for you to balance your spiritual Self and the material Self, which means the part of you that is beautifully peaceful and balanced and in unity. That is unity of the Your Essence - Soul with The Great Spirit, that energy that is greater than the Self, as well as the material part of your life, your relationships and family, career, money and possessions. To be in touch with the Soul means transcendence of the ego.

The material aspect of your life is at your own discretion, your choice. The spiritual side has to be actively sought by yourself. It is not taught in schools or something that you experience through the growing up process. It is learned gradually through spiritual enquiry and spiritual experience. If you are lucky enough to have spiritual teachers around you, spiritual parents, perhaps, then the seeking may start early. However for many it is something that starts later on in life, when the material world has lost its allure.

Thanks

For this book I would like to thank the following, whom I consider to be great Teachers and Healers: Trudi Morgan in Devon, Carol Holly in Sussex, Swami Satchidananda Ma in Hampshire, Gilly Towers in Surrey, Eagle's Wing - Dawn Russell, Lorraine Grayston and Leo Rutherford from Sussex and Alison Pollock in Surrey.

Please visit Michelle's website at www.purplebuddha.co.uk

Michelle's book *Your Quest for a Spiritual Life* and Meditation CD *Your Quest for Peace, Healing & Balance* are available from the website.

B O O K S

O is a symbol of the world, of oneness and unity. In different cultures it also means the "eye," symbolizing knowledge and insight. We aim to publish books that are accessible, constructive and that challenge accepted opinion, both that of academia and the "moral majority."

Our books are available in all good English language bookstores worldwide. If you don't see the book on the shelves ask the bookstore to order it for you, quoting the ISBN number and title. Alternatively you can order online (all major online retail sites carry our titles) or contact the distributor in the relevant country, listed on the copyright page.

See our website www.o-books.net for a full list of over 500 titles, growing by 100 a year.

And tune in to myspiritradio.com for our book review radio show, hosted by June-Elleni Laine, where you can listen to the authors discussing their books.